Annuals *for* Alberta

Laura Peters
Donna Dawson

2007 by Lone Pine Publishing
First printed in 2007   10 9 8 7 6 5 4 3 2 1
Printed in China

The Publisher: Lone Pine Publishing
10145 – 81 Avenue   1808 – B Street NW, Suite 140
Edmonton, AB, Canada T6E 1W9   Auburn, WA, USA 98001

Website: www.lonepinepublishing.com

Library and Archives Canada Cataloguing in Publication

Peters, Laura, 1968–
    Annuals for Alberta / Laura Peters, Donna Dawson.

Includes index.
ISBN–13: 978–1–55105–351–6

    1. Annuals (Plants)—Alberta. 2. Gardening—Alberta.
I. Dawson, Donna, 1951- II. Title.
SB422.P38 2007   635.9'312097123   C2006–903175–4

Editorial Director: Nancy Foulds
Project Editor: Sandra Bit
Photo Co-ordinator: Don Williamson
Production Manager: Gene Longson
Book Design & Layout: Heather Markham
Production Support: Trina Koscielnuk, Elliot Engley
Cover Design: Gerry Dotto
Photo Scanning: Elite Lithographers Co.

Photography: All photographs by Tim Matheson, Tamara Eder and Laura Peters with the following exceptions: AAS selection 119b, 214a&c, 215a&b; Doris Baucom 211a; David Cavagnaro 16c, 91b, 115; Elliot Engley 25a, 26, 27a&b, 28a,b&c; EuroAmerican 67a, 139a; Jen Fafard 143b; Derek Fell 91a, 117a, 125b, 185a, 195a, 196b, 197a, 231a; Erika Flatt 76–77, 81b; Anne Gordon 105a, 114; Horticolor 110; Horticultural Photography: Arthur N. Orans 105b; Debra Knapke 146a, 156; Janet Loughrey 60, 61; Kim Patrick O'Leary 14, 25c, 104, 108a, 117b, 119a, 149a&b, 164, 183b, 257b; Allison Penko 35c, 56c, 80, 81a, 82a, 83, 105a, 124, 125a, 132, 133a&b, 192; Robert Ritchie 39, 41b, 43b; Joy Spurr 111a; Peter Thompstone 56a, 87a, 112, 113a, 123b, 145b, 162a&b, 163a, 187b, 241a&b; Don Williamson 74, 118a, 126, 127a&b; Carol Woo 37.

We acknowledge the financial support of the Government of Canada through the Book Publishing Industry Development Program (BPIDP) for our publishing activities.

PC: *P13*

Contents

4

Acknowledgements

I would like to thank my parents, Gary and Lucy Peters, and my close friends, but I would especially like to send out a big thank you to Christopher, my biggest fan. Your support and encouragement mean the world to me. A special thanks to Donna Dawson for her love of gardening and her giving nature. I would also like to acknowledge those fellow Albertans who have approached me over the years to share their love of gardening, and more so, to share their desire for gardening books written about Alberta by an Albertan. I hope this book, along with the other Alberta books in this series inspire you to experiment, to have fun and to enjoy everything that gardening on the prairies has to offer. I'll never get bored of hearing about gardeners visiting their local garden centre with this book tucked under their arm, flagged with stickies and dog-eared from frequent use. Happy gardening to all and let's continue to keep our communities blooming! *Laura Peters*

An annual is by definition a plant whose life cycle lasts only one year from seed to bloom, and hopefully to seed again. Here in Alberta, with our long days of sun, we are able to plant a huge variety of annuals for our enjoyment. Whether in garden beds or containers, annuals offer us continuous colour when our perennials fade. This book will not only help you choose the right plant for the right place, it will also show you how to prepare for them, look after them and enjoy them until frost. My sincere thanks to Laura, who has put a great deal of effort into this wonderfully easy book to use and reference often. *Donna Dawson*

The Flowers at a Glance

A PICTORIAL GUIDE IN ALPHABETICAL ORDER, BY COMMON NAME

African Daisy
p. 48

Ageratum
p. 50

Amaranth
p. 54

Angelonia
p. 58

Asarina
p. 60

Baby's Breath
p. 62

Bachelor's Buttons
p. 64

Bacopa
p. 66

Beefsteak Plant
p. 68

Bidens
p. 70

California Poppy
p. 72

Calla Lily
p. 74

Candytuft
p. 78

Canna Lily
p. 82

Cape Daisy
p. 84

China Aster
p. 86

Cigar Flower
p. 88

Cleome
p. 92

Clover
p. 96

Cobbitty Daisy
p. 98

Coleus
p. 100

Corn Cockle
p. 104

Cosmos
p. 106

Cup-and-Saucer Vine
p. 110

Cup Flower
p. 112

Dahlberg Daisy
p. 114

Dianthus
p. 116

Dwarf Morning Glory
p. 120

Fan Flower
p. 122

Feverfew
p. 124

Flowering Flax
p. 126

Flowering Maple
p. 128

Forget-Me-Not
p. 130

Fountain Grass
p. 132

Four-O'Clock Flower
p. 134

Fuchsia
p. 136

Gaura
p. 140

Geranium
p. 144

Gazania
p. 142

Globe Amaranth
p. 148

Godetia
p. 150

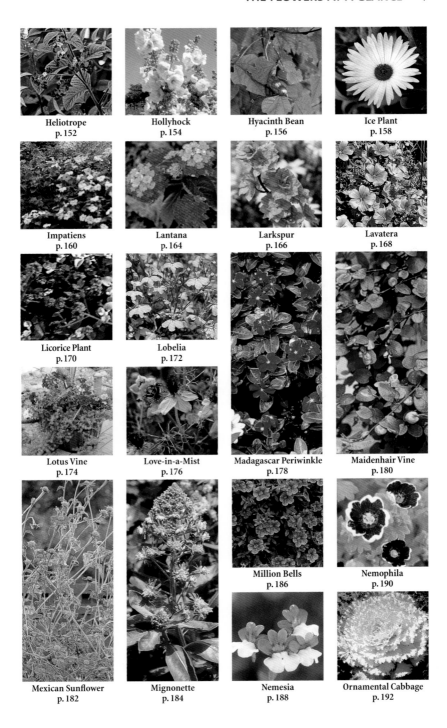

Heliotrope
p. 152

Hollyhock
p. 154

Hyacinth Bean
p. 156

Ice Plant
p. 158

Impatiens
p. 160

Lantana
p. 164

Larkspur
p. 166

Lavatera
p. 168

Licorice Plant
p. 170

Lobelia
p. 172

Lotus Vine
p. 174

Love-in-a-Mist
p. 176

Madagascar Periwinkle
p. 178

Maidenhair Vine
p. 180

Mexican Sunflower
p. 182

Mignonette
p. 184

Million Bells
p. 186

Nemophila
p. 190

Nemesia
p. 188

Ornamental Cabbage
p. 192

Osteospermum
p. 194

Oxalis
p. 198

Painted-Tongue
p. 200

Pansy
p. 202

Passion Flower
p. 206

Pentas
p. 208

Persian Shield
p. 210

Petunia
p. 212

Pimpernel
p. 216

Pincushion Flower
p. 218

Poppy
p. 220

Portulaca
p. 224

Salvia
p. 226

Silene
p. 230

Snapdragon
p. 232

Statice
p. 236

Stock
p. 238

Strawflower
p. 240

Sunflower
p. 242

Swan River Daisy
p. 246

Sweet Pea
p. 250

Toadflax
p. 254

Sweet Alyssum
p. 248

Sweet Potato Vine
p. 252

Verbena
p. 256

Vinca
p. 260

Wishbone Flower
p. 262

Zinnia
p. 264

Introduction

True annuals are plants that germinate, mature, bloom, set seed and die in one growing season. The plants we treat as annuals, or bedding plants, may be annuals, biennials or tender perennials. Our expectation is to plant them in the spring or summer and enjoy them for only one growing season. Many biennials, if started early enough, will flower the year you plant them, and many plants that are perennial in warmer climates will grow and flower before they succumb to our cold winter temperatures.

Annuals provide long-lasting colour and fill in spaces in garden beds. Most annuals are started indoors and then transplanted into the garden after the last spring frost, but some can be sown directly in the garden. A sure sign of spring's arrival is the rush of gardeners to local garden centres, greenhouses and farmers' markets to pick out their new annuals.

Climate, Geography & Soil

Alberta, one of Canada's sunniest provinces, experiences annual bright sunshine totals between 1900 and 2500 hours per year. Northern Alberta receives about 18 hours of daylight in the summer. The long summer days make summer the sunniest season of the year in Alberta. Along with our warm sunny days are cooler nights. Most annuals prefer this balance in order to thrive all summer long, making the climate in Alberta excellent for growing them.

Temperatures are generally higher in southern than northern Alberta. In July, the average daily temperature ranges from warmer than 18° C (65° F) in the south to cooler than 13° C (55° F) in the Rocky Mountains and the north. In January, the average daily temperature ranges from cooler than -24° C (-11° F) in the far north to warmer than -10° C (14° F) in the south and the mountains. The warming effect of the Chinook winds near the mountains produces a west to east trend in winter temperatures.

In Alberta the last spring frost occurs anywhere from mid- to late May (see map, p. 12), and the first fall frost generally comes in September. Alberta gardeners can expect a frost-free period of about four to five months, which gives annuals plenty of time to mature and fill the garden with abundant colour. If a specific spring or fall is warmer than usual, gardeners can make additional plantings and enjoy annuals a little longer.

Rainfall is fairly reliable in most parts of Alberta, and with good mulch to prevent water loss, most plants will usually need moderate supplemental watering, depending on the weather. Precipitation is generally highest along the mountains and into west central Alberta. Precipitation from early May to late August varies from just under 200 mm (8") in the driest prairie areas to more than 325 mm (13") in the mountains. From early September to late April, precipitation ranges from less than 150 mm (6") in the driest prairie region to more than 275 mm (11") in the mountains. In a dry year, Alberta may receive no significant rainfall throughout the summer. In these years, supplemental watering will be necessary.

AVERAGE LAST-FROST
DATE MAP

ALBERTA
LAST SPRING FROST DATES

BEFORE MAY 21
MAY 21 – MAY 31
MAY 31 – JUNE 11
JUNE 11 – JUNE 21
JUNE 21 – JULY 1
AFTER JULY 1

AVERAGE FIRST-FROST
DATE MAP

ALBERTA
FIRST FALL FROST DATES
BEFORE SEPTEMBER 1
SEPTEMBER 1 – SEPTEMBER 11
SEPTEMBER 11 – SEPTEMBER 21
AFTER SEPTEMBER 21

Why Plant Annuals?

Annuals are popular because they produce lots of flowers, in a wide variety of colours, over a long period of time. Many annuals bloom from spring right through to early fall. Beyond this basic appeal, gardeners are constantly finding new ways to include annuals in their gardens, using them to accent areas in an established border, featuring them as the main attraction in a new garden or combining them with other plants. Many annuals are adapted to a variety of growing conditions, from hot, dry sun to cool, damp shade. They are fun for beginners and experienced gardeners alike and, because annuals are temporary and relatively inexpensive, they can be easily replaced if they are past their prime.

Dahlias and gazanias (foreground) Ageratum (background)

Some of the most popular, easy to grow and reliable annuals include geraniums, petunias and impatiens, but the selection increases every year. New species have been introduced from other parts of the world. There are new and sometimes improved varieties of old favourites with expanded colour ranges or increased pest resistance. With the increased interest in organic gardening, and in response to concerns about over-hybridization, the use of native plants and heritage varieties is on the upswing.

Marigolds, impatiens, million bells and dahlias

Some new varieties may experience a short period of popularity, but fail to meet gardeners' expectations and fall by the wayside. Others join the ranks of the favourites. Greatly improved varieties that have been tried in gardens across Canada and the United States may be chosen by members of the horticultural industry as 'All-America Selections Winners.' These outstanding plants are the most widely known and frequently grown. They usually carry the AASW seal and are worth seeking out.

Annuals look great in containers.

Annual Gardens

The short life of annuals allows gardeners flexibility and freedom when planning a garden. Whereas trees and shrubs form the permanent structure or the 'bones' of the garden, and perennials and groundcovers fill the spaces between them, annuals add bold patterns and bright splashes of colour. Include annuals anywhere you would like some variety and dazzle—in pots staggered up porch steps or on a deck, in windowsill planters or in hanging baskets. Even well-established gardens are brightened and given a new look with the addition of annual flowers.

Something as simple as a planting of impatiens under a tree can be different each year with different varieties and colour combinations. When planning your garden, consult as many sources as you can. Look through gardening books and ask friends and greenhouse experts for advice. Notice what you like or dislike about various gardens, and make a list of the plants you would like to include in your garden.

You can create whatever style garden you desire by cleverly mixing annuals. A tidy, symmetrical, formal garden can be enhanced by adding a few types of annuals or by choosing annuals of the same flower colour. In the same garden, adding many different species and colours of annuals relaxes the neat plantings of trees and shrubs. An informal, cottage-style garden can be a riot of plants and colours.

When choosing annuals, most people make the colour, size and shape of the flowers their prime considerations. Other aspects to consider are the size and shape of the plant and leaves. A variety of flower, plant and leaf sizes, shapes and colours will make your garden more interesting. Consult the individual plant entries and the Quick Reference Chart on p. 266.

Colours have different effects on our senses. Cool colours, such as purple, blue and green, are soothing and relaxing and can make a small garden appear larger. Some annuals with cool colours are lobelia, ageratum and angelonia. Warm colours, such as red, orange and yellow, are more stimulating and appear to fill larger spaces. Warm colours can make even the largest, most imposing garden seem warm and welcoming. Annuals with warm colours include California poppy and gazania.

If you have time to enjoy your garden mainly in the evenings, you may want to consider pale colours such as white and yellow. These show up well at dusk and even at night. Some plants, such as evening-scented stock, have flowers that are most fragrant as night falls and that add an attractive dimension to the evening garden.

Foliage colour varies a great deal as well. Some annuals are grown for their interesting or colourful foliage and not for the flowers at all, yet some plants have interesting foliage and flowers. Leaves come in almost every imaginable shade of green and also in a range of other colours including red, purple, yellow, blue and bronze. Some foliage is variegated, that is, patterned or with veins that contrast with the colour of the leaves. Some foliage plants, such as coleus, are used by themselves, while others, such as dusty miller, provide an interesting backdrop for brightly coloured flowers.

ANNUALS WITH INTERESTING FOLIAGE

- Ice Plant
- Lotus Vine
- Coleus
- Licorice Plant
- Ornamental Cabbage
- Persian Shield
- Sweet Potato Vine

Sweet potato vine

Ageratum provides cool colour.
California poppies provide warm colour.

Texture is another important element to consider. Both foliage and flowers have a visual texture. Large leaves appear coarse in texture and can make a garden appear smaller and more shaded. Coarse-textured flowers appear bold and dramatic and can be seen from far away. Small leaves appear fine in texture and create a sense of increased space and light. Fine-textured flowers appear soothing. Sometimes the flowers and foliage of a plant have contrasting textures. Using a variety of textures helps make a garden interesting and appealing.

FINE-TEXTURED ANNUALS

Sweet Alyssum
Bacopa
Dahlberg Daisy
Larkspur
Lobelia
Love-in-a-Mist
Swan River Daisy

COARSE-TEXTURED ANNUALS

Cleome
Mexican Sunflower
Hollyhock
Geranium (scented)
Sunflower
Verbena

Sunflower

Dahlberg daisy

Hollyhock

Larkspur

Getting Started

Before you start shopping for or planting your annuals, consider the growing conditions in each area of your garden. For your plants to thrive, it's important that their specific needs be coordinated with the microenvironments in your garden. Plants will be healthier and less susceptible to problems if grown in their preferred conditions. It is difficult to significantly modify your garden's existing conditions; match the plants to the garden instead. Consult the individual plant entries and the Quick Reference Chart on p. 266.

The levels of light, the porosity, pH and texture of soil, the amount of exposure in your garden and the plants' tolerance to frost provide guidelines for selecting your plants. Sketching your garden will help you visualize the various conditions. Note any shaded, low-lying, wet, exposed or windy areas. Understanding your garden's growing conditions will help you learn to recognize which plants will perform best, saving you money and time. Conversely, experimenting with different annuals will help you learn about the conditions of your garden.

Light

Four levels of light may be present in a garden: full sun, partial shade (partial sun), light shade and full shade. Available light is affected by buildings, trees, fences and the position of the sun at different times of the day and year. Knowing what light is available in your garden will help you determine where to place each plant.

Plants in full sun locations, such as along south-facing walls, receive direct sunlight for six or more hours a day. Partial shade locations, such as east- or west-facing walls, receive direct sunlight

get scorched leaves or even wilt and die if they get too much sun. Many other plants tolerate a wide range of light conditions.

ANNUALS FOR SUN
- African Daisy
- Bidens
- Cosmos
- Geranium
- Globe Amaranth
- Heliotrope
- Portulaca
- Statice
- Sunflower

ANNUALS FOR SHADE
- Godetia
- Coleus
- Impatiens
- Fuchsia
- Pansy

ANNUALS FOR ANY LIGHT
- Coleus
- Cup Flower
- Fan Flower
- Lobelia
- New Guinea Impatiens
- Godetia
- Nemophila

for part of the day and shade for the rest. Light shade locations receive shade for most or all of the day, but some light filters through to ground level. For example, the ground underneath a small-leaved tree, such as a birch, is often lightly shaded. Full shade locations, which would include the north side of a house, receive no direct sunlight.

Sun-loving plants may become tall and straggly and flower poorly in too much shade. Shade-loving plants may

Coleus (above), lobelia (below)

Soil

Good soil is an extremely important element of a healthy garden. Plant roots rely on the air, water and nutrients that are held within soil. Plants also depend on soil to hold them upright. The soil, in turn, benefits in at least three ways: plant roots improve soil texture by breaking down large particles; plants prevent soil erosion by reducing the amount of exposed surface and by binding together small particles with their roots; and plants increase soil fertility when they die and

Fuchsia

break down, adding organic nutrients to the soil and feeding beneficial microorganisms.

Soil is made up of particles of different sizes. Sand particles are the largest. Water drains quickly from sandy soil and nutrients tend to get washed away. Sandy soil does not compact very easily because the large particles leave air pockets between them. Clay particles, which are the smallest, can be seen only through a microscope. Clay holds the most nutrients, but it also compacts easily and has little air space. Clay is slow to absorb water and equally slow to let it drain. Silt is midway in size between sand and clay. Most soils are composed of a combination of these different particle sizes and are called loams.

It is important to consider the pH level (acidity or alkalinity) of soil, which influences the availability of nutrients. Most plants thrive in soil with a pH between 5.5 and 7.5. Soil pH varies a great deal from place to place in Alberta. Kits for testing the pH of

soil can be purchased at most garden centres, but soil-testing labs can fully analyze the pH as well as the quantities of various nutrients in your soil much more accurately. They'll often recommend how to correct any imbalances as well. The acidity of soil can be reduced by adding horticultural lime or wood ashes and increased by adding sulfur, peat moss or pine needles. If you are trying to grow plants that require soil with a pH quite different than that in your garden, consider growing them in a planter or raised bed where it is easier to control and alter the pH level of soil.

Drainage, the ability of water to move through soil, is affected by soil type and terrain in your garden. Gravelly soil on a hillside will drain very quickly, while low-lying areas may drain very slowly, if at all. Water retention can be improved by adding organic matter. Drainage may be improved in wet areas by installing a drainage system, by adding sand or gravel or by building raised beds.

Cleome (above), four-o'clock flower (centre)

Mexican sunflower (below)

ANNUALS FOR MOIST SOIL
Cleome
Lavatera
Pansy
Forget-Me-Not
Four-O'Clock Flower

ANNUALS FOR DRY SOIL
African Daisy
Cosmos
Ice Plant
Portulaca
Mexican Sunflower
Statice

Exposure

Your garden is exposed to wind, heat, cold and rain, and some plants are better adapted than others to withstand the potential damage of these forces. Buildings, walls, fences, hills, hedges, trees and even tall perennials influence and often reduce exposure.

Wind and heat are the most likely elements to damage annuals. The sun can be very intense, and heat can rise quickly on a sunny afternoon. Plant annuals that tolerate or even thrive in hot weather in the hot spots in your garden.

Moss-lined hanging baskets are especially susceptible to wind and heat exposure, losing water from the soil surface and the leaves. Water can evaporate from all sides of a moss basket, and in hot or windy locations moisture can be depleted very quickly. Hanging baskets look wonderful, but watch for wilting, and water the baskets regularly to keep them looking great.

Overwatering or too much rain can also be damaging. Early in the season, seeds or seedlings can be washed away in heavy rain; mulch around the seeded area will help prevent this problem. Established annuals, or their flowers, can be beaten down by heavy rain.

Most annuals will recover, but some, such as petunias, are slow to do so. Place sensitive annuals in protected areas, or choose plants or varieties that are quick to recover from rain damage. Many of the small-flowered petunia varieties now available are quick to recover from heavy rain. Painted tongue does best with shelter from wind and heavy rain.

Frost Tolerance

When planting annuals, consider their ability to tolerate an unexpected frost. The dates for last frost and first frost vary greatly from region to region in North America. Most Alberta gardeners can expect a chance of frost until mid- to late May if not early June. The map on p. 12 gives a general idea of when you can expect your last frost. Keep in mind that these dates can vary significantly from year to year and within the general regions. Your local garden centre should be able to provide more precise information on frost expectations for your area.

Annuals are grouped into three categories based on how they tolerate cold weather: hardy, half-hardy or tender. Consult the Quick Reference Chart on p. 266 for hardiness categories of annuals in this book.

Hardy annuals can tolerate low temperatures and even frost. They can be planted in the garden early and may continue to flower long into fall or even winter. Many hardy annuals are sown directly in the garden before the last frost date. Half-hardy annuals can tolerate a light frost but will be killed by a heavy one. These annuals, generally started early from seed indoors, can be planted out around the last-frost date. Bachelor's buttons is a half-hardy annual.

Tender annuals have no frost tolerance at all and might suffer if the temperatures drop to a few degrees above freezing. For example, nasturtiums become a soggy mess after a light frost. Tender plants are often started early indoors and not planted in the garden until the last frost date has passed and the ground has had a chance to warm up. The advantage to these annuals is that they often tolerate hot summer temperatures.

Protecting plants from frost is relatively simple. Plants can be covered overnight with sheets, towels, burlap or even cardboard boxes. Don't use plastic because it doesn't retain heat and therefore doesn't provide plants with any insulation.

Painted-tongue

Preparing the Garden

Taking the time to properly prepare your flowerbeds will save you time and effort over the summer. Give your annuals a good start with weeded soil that has had organic material added. For container gardens, use potting soil because regular garden soil loses its structure when used in pots, quickly compacting into a solid mass that drains poorly.

Loosen the soil with a large garden fork and remove the weeds. Avoid working the soil when it is very wet or very dry because you will damage the soil structure by breaking down the pockets that hold air and water.

Organic matter is an important component of soil. It increases the water-holding and nutrient-holding capacity of sandy soil and binds together the large particles. It increases the water-absorbing and draining potential of clay soil by opening up spaces between the tiny particles. Common organic additives for your soil include grass clippings, shredded leaves, peat moss, chopped straw, well-rotted manure and composted bark.

When preparing an area for planting, it is advisable to add a 7.5–10cm (3–4") layer of organic matter and work it into the soil with a spade or rototiller. To determine how much organic matter you need to provide a 7.5–10cm (3–4") layer, use the following equation:

Compute area by multiplying length of garden bed by width (for example, 6' × 18' = 108 sq. ft. or 2m × 5m=10 sq. m).

Multiply area by inches of depth wanted (108 sq. ft. × 4" = 432 sq. ft. or 10 sq. m × 0.1m=1 cu. m).

Divide by 12 to get the amount in cu. ft. (432 ÷ 12 = 36 cu. ft.).

Because 27 cu. ft. equals 1 cu. yd., you would need 1 ⅓ cu. yd. of organic matter to provide a 4" layer to an area of 108 sq. ft. If measuring in metric, you will need 1 cu. m of organic matter to provide a 0.1 m (10 cm) layer of organic matter to an area the size of 10 sq. m.

Composting

Any organic matter you add will be of greater benefit to your soil if it has been composted first. In natural environments, such as forests or meadows, compost is created when leaves, plant bits and other debris are broken down on the soil surface. This process will also take place in your garden beds if you work fresh organic matter into the soil. However, microorganisms that break down organic matter use the same nutrients as your plants. The tougher the organic matter, the more nutrients in the soil will be used trying to break the matter down. As a result, your plants will be robbed of vital nutrients, particularly nitrogen. Also, adding fresh organic matter, such as garden debris, might encourage or introduce pests and diseases in your garden.

A compost pile or bin, which can be either built or purchased already assembled, creates a controlled environment where organic matter can be fully broken down before being added to your garden.

One kind of composting bin

Creating compost is a simple process. Kitchen scraps, grass clippings and fall leaves will slowly break down if left in a pile. The process can be sped up by following a few simple guidelines.

Your compost pile should contain both dry and fresh materials, with a larger proportion of dry matter such as chopped straw, shredded leaves or sawdust. Fresh green matter, such as vegetable scraps, grass clippings or pulled weeds, breaks down quickly and produces nitrogen, which feeds the decomposer organisms while they break down the tougher dry matter.

Layer the green matter with the dry matter and mix in small amounts of garden soil or previously finished compost. The addition of soil or compost will introduce beneficial microorganisms. If the pile seems very dry, sprinkle some water between the layers—the compost should be moist like a wrung-out sponge, but not soaking wet. Adding nitrogen, like that found in fertilizer, will speed up decomposition. Avoid strong concentrations that can kill beneficial organisms.

Each week or two, use a pitchfork to turn the pile over or poke holes into it. This will help aerate the material, which will speed up decomposition. A compost pile that is kept aerated can generate a lot of heat—71° C (160° F) or more. Such high temperatures destroy weed seeds and kill many damaging organisms. Most beneficial organisms are not killed until the temperature rises higher than 71° C (160° F). To monitor the temperature of the compost near the middle of the pile you will need a thermometer that is attached to a long probe, similar to a large meat thermometer. Turn your compost when the temperature reaches 71° C (160° F). Aerating the pile will stimulate the process to heat up again but prevent the temperatures from becoming high enough to kill the beneficial organisms.

Avoid adding any pest or disease-ridden materials to your compost pile. If the damaging organisms are not destroyed, they could be spread throughout your garden. If you do add material you suspect of harboring pests or diseases, add it near the centre of the pile where the temperature is highest.

When you can no longer recognize the matter that you put into the compost bin, and the temperature no longer rises upon turning, your compost is ready to be mixed into your garden beds. Getting to this point can take as little as one month and will leave you with organic material that is rich in nutrients and beneficial organisms.

Compost can also be purchased from most garden centres.

Selecting Annuals

Many gardeners consider the trip to the local garden centre to pick out their annual plants an important rite of spring. Other gardeners find it rewarding to start their own annuals from seed. There are benefits to both methods, and many gardeners choose to use a combination of the two. Purchasing annuals provides you with plants that are well grown and often already in bloom, which is useful if you don't have the room or the facilities to start seeds. Some seeds require specific conditions that are difficult to achieve in a house or they have erratic germination rates, which makes starting them yourself impractical. On the other hand, starting from seed may offer you a greater selection of species and varieties, because seed catalogues often list many more plants than are offered at garden centres. Starting annuals from seed is discussed on p. 26.

Purchased annual plants are grown in a variety of containers. Some are sold in individual pots, some in divided cell-packs and others in undivided trays. Each type has advantages and disadvantages.

Annuals in individual pots are usually well established and have plenty of space for root growth. These annuals have probably been seeded in flat trays and then transplanted into individual pots once they developed a few leaves. The cost of labour, pots and soil can make this option more expensive. If you are planting a large area you may also find it difficult to transport large numbers of plants.

Annuals in cell-packs are often inexpensive and hold several plants, making them easy to transport. These annuals suffer less root damage when transplanted than do annuals in undivided trays, but because each cell is quite small, plants may become root-bound quickly.

Annuals in undivided trays have plenty of room for root growth and can be left in the trays longer than in other types of containers. Their roots, however, tend to become entangled, making the plants difficult to separate.

Regardless of the type of container, the best plants to choose are often not yet flowering. These plants are younger and are less likely to be root-bound. Check for roots emerging from the holes at the bottom of the cells, or gently remove the plant from the container to look at the roots. Too many roots means that the plant is too mature for the container, especially if the roots are wrapped around the inside of the container in a thick web. Such plants are slow to establish once they are transplanted into the garden.

Root-bound seedling (left), nicely rooted plant (right)

The plants should be compact and have good colour. Healthy leaves look firm and vibrant. Unhealthy leaves may be wilted, chewed or discoloured. Tall, leggy plants have likely been deprived of light. Sickly plants may not survive being transplanted and may spread pests or diseases to the rest of your garden.

Once you get your annuals home, water them if they are dry. Annuals growing in small containers may require water more than once a day. Begin to harden off the plants so they can be transplanted into the garden as soon as possible. Your annuals are probably accustomed to growing in the sheltered environment of a greenhouse, and they will need to get used to the climate outdoors. Place them outdoors in a lightly shaded spot each day and move them into a sheltered porch, garage or house each night for about a week. This process will acclimatize them to your garden.

Fuchsia (centre) and lantana (below) are often only available as transplants.

Annuals from Seed

Starting annuals from seed can be fun and can provide you with a wider variety of annuals than that available as bedding plants. Dozens of catalogues from different growers offer a diverse selection of annuals that can be started from seed. Many gardeners while away chilly winter evenings by poring over seed catalogues and planning their spring and summer gardens.

Starting your own annuals can save you money, particularly if you need a lot of plants. The basic equipment necessary is not expensive, and most seeds can be started in a sunny window. However, you may encounter the problem of limited space. One or two trays of annuals don't take up too much room, but starting more than that may be unreasonable. For this reason, many gardeners start a few specialty plants themselves but purchase the bulk of their annuals as plants from a garden centre.

Each plant in this book will have specific information on starting it from seed, but a few basic steps can be followed for all seeds. The easiest way for the home gardener to start seeds is to use cell-packs in trays with plastic dome covers. The cell-packs keep roots separated, and the tray and dome keep moisture in.

Seeds can also be started in pots, peat pots or peat pellets. The advantage to starting in peat pots or pellets is that you will not disturb the roots when you transplant your annuals. When planting peat pots into the garden, be sure to remove the top couple of inches of pot. If any of the pot sticks up out of the soil, it can wick moisture away from the roots.

Use a growing mix or soil mix intended for seedlings. These mixes are very fine, usually made from peat moss, vermiculite and perlite. The mix will have good water-holding capacity and will have been sterilized to prevent pests and diseases from attacking your tender young seedlings. Fill your pots or seed trays with the soil mix and firm it down slightly. Soil that is too firmly packed will not drain well. Wet the soil before planting your seeds to prevent them from getting washed around. The easiest method is to wet the soil before you fill the trays or pots.

Large seeds can be planted one or two to a cell, but smaller seeds may have to be placed in a folded piece of paper and sprinkled evenly over the soil surface. Very tiny seeds, like those of petunia, can be mixed with fine sand before being sprinkled across the soil surface.

Small seeds will not need to be covered with any more soil, but medium-sized seeds can be lightly covered with soil, and large seeds can be poked into the soil. Some seeds need to be exposed to light in order to germinate; these should be left on the soil surface regardless of their size.

Place pots or flats of seeds in plastic bags to retain humidity while the seeds are germinating. Many planting trays come with clear plastic covers, which can be placed over the trays to keep the moisture in. Remove the plastic once the seeds have germinated.

Water seeds and small seedlings with a fine spray from a hand-held mister—small seeds can easily be washed around if the spray is too strong. At one greenhouse, where the seed trays containing sweet alyssum were once watered a little too vigorously, sweet alyssum was soon found growing just about everywhere—with other plants, in the gravel on the floor, even in some of the flowerbeds outside. The lesson is 'water gently.' A less hardy species would not have come up at all if its seeds were washed into an adverse location.

Seeds provide all the energy and nutrients that young seedlings require. Small seedlings will not need to be fertilized until they have about four or five true leaves. True leaves are the ones that look like the mature leaves. (The first one or two leaves are the cotyledons, or seed leaves.) When the first leaves that sprouted (the seed leaves) begin to shrivel, the plant has used up all its seed energy. You can then begin to use fertilizer diluted to one-quarter strength when feeding seedlings or young plants.

Preparing seed trays

Using folded paper to plant small seeds

Watering seeds with a mister

Prepared seed tray

Take care to prevent damping off, a disease caused by soil-borne fungi. An afflicted seedling appears to have been pinched at soil level. The pinched area blackens and the seedling topples over and dies. Sterile soil mix, evenly moist soil and good air circulation will help prevent this problem.

If the seedlings get too big for their containers before you are ready to plant them out, you may have to pot them to prevent them from becoming root-bound. Harden plants off by exposing them to outdoor conditions for increas-ing periods of time every day for at least a week before planting them out.

To start seeds directly in the garden, begin with a well-prepared bed that has been smoothly raked. The small fur-rows left by the rake will help hold moisture and prevent the seeds from being washed away. Sprinkle the seeds into the furrows and cover them lightly with peat moss or more soil. Larger seeds can be planted slightly deeper into the soil. You may not want to sow very tiny seeds directly in the garden because they can blow or wash away.

Sprouted seedlings with fluorescent light

The soil should be kept moist to ensure even germination. Use a gentle spray to avoid washing the seeds around the bed or they will pool into dense clumps. Covering your newly seeded bed with chicken wire, an old sheet or some thorny branches will discourage animals from digging.

ANNUALS FOR DIRECT SEEDING

- Baby's Breath
- Bachelor's Buttons
- California Poppy
- Candytuft
- Cleome
- Cosmos
- Larkspur
- Lavatera
- Love-in-a-Mist
- Poppy

Poppy (above)

Candytuft (centre), bachelor's buttons (below)

Sweet pea (above)

Planting Annuals

Once your annuals are hardened off, it is time to plant them out. If your beds are already prepared, you are ready to start. The only tool you are likely to need is a trowel. Be sure you have set aside enough time to do the job. You don't want to have young plants out of their pots and not finish planting them. If they are left out in the sun, they can quickly dry out and die. To prevent this problem, choose an overcast day for planting.

If you have not prepared a flower bed by adding organic matter (see the section on Preparing the Garden, p. 22), add a trowelful of compost to the planting hole and mix it into the garden soil before adding your annual.

Moisten the soil to help remove the plants from their containers more easily. Push on the bottom of the cell or pot with your thumb to ease the plants out. If the plants were growing in an undivided tray, then you will have to gently untangle the roots. If the roots are very tangled, immerse them in water and wash some of the soil away to help free the plants from one another. If you must handle the plant, hold it by a leaf to avoid crushing the stems. Remove and discard any damaged leaves or growth.

The rootball should contain a network of white plant roots. If the rootball is densely matted and twisted, break it apart in order to encourage the roots to extend and grow outward. Do so by breaking apart the tangles a bit with your thumbs. New root growth will start from the breaks, allowing the plant to spread outwards.

Insert your trowel into the soil and pull it towards you, creating a wedge. Place your annual into the hole and firm the soil around the plant with your hands. Water newly planted annuals gently but thoroughly. Until they are established they will need regular watering for a few weeks.

You don't have to be conservative when arranging your flowerbeds. Though formal bedding-out patterns are still used in many parks and gardens, plantings can be made in casual groups and natural drifts. The quickest way to space out your annuals is to remove them from their containers and randomly place them on the bed. You can then mix colours and plants without too much planning. Plant a small section at a time—don't allow the roots to dry out. This is especially important if you have a large bed to plant.

If you are adding just a few annuals here and there to accent your shrub and perennial plantings, plant in groups. Random clusters of three to five plants add colour and interest.

Combine low-growing or spreading annuals with tall or bushy ones. Keep

Informal planting (above), formal planting (below)

the tallest plants towards the back and smallest plants towards the front of the bed. Doing so improves the visibility of the plants and hides the often unattractive lower limbs of taller plants. Be sure to leave your plants enough room to spread. They may look lonely and far apart when you first plant them, but annuals will quickly grow to fill in the space.

Caring for Annuals

Some annuals require more care than others do, but most require minimal care once established. Weeding, watering, fertilizing and deadheading are the basic tasks that, when performed regularly, will keep your garden looking its best. As well, some plants grown as annuals are actually perennials and may be overwintered with little effort.

Weeding

Controlling weed populations keeps the garden healthy and neat. Weeding may not be anyone's favourite task, but it is essential. Weeds compete with your plants for light, nutrients and space, and they can harbour pests and diseases.

Weeds can be pulled by hand or with a hoe. Shortly after a rainfall, when the soil is soft and damp, is the easiest time to pull weeds. A hoe scuffed quickly across the soil surface will uproot small weeds and sever larger ones from their roots. Try to pull weeds out while they are still small. Once they are large enough to flower, many will quickly set seed; then you will have an entire new generation to worry about.

Mulching

A layer of mulch around your plants will help keep weeds from germinating by preventing sufficient light from reaching the seeds. Those that do germinate will be smothered or will find it difficult to get to the soil surface, exhausting their energy before getting a chance to grow.

Mulch also helps maintain consistent soil temperatures and ensures that moisture is retained more effectively. In areas that receive heavy wind or rainfall, mulch can protect the soil and prevent erosion. Mulching is effective in both garden beds and planters.

Organic mulches include such materials as compost, bark chips, grass clippings or shredded leaves. These mulches add nutrients to soil as they break down, thus improving the quality of the soil and ultimately the health of your plants.

Spread about 5–8 cm (2–3") of mulch over the soil after you have planted your annuals. Don't pile the mulch too thickly immediately around the crowns and stems of your annuals. Mulching right up against plants traps moisture and prevents air circulation, encouraging fungal disease.

As your mulch breaks down over summer, be sure to replenish it.

Containers require regular watering.

Watering

Water thoroughly but infrequently. Annuals given a light sprinkle of water every day will develop roots that stay close to the soil surface, making the plants vulnerable to heat and dry spells. Annuals given a deep watering once a week will develop a deeper root system. In a dry spell they will be adapted to seeking out the water trapped deeper in the ground.

Be sure the water penetrates at least 10 cm (4") into the soil; this is equal to 2.5 cm (1") of applied water. More water may be needed in very hot weather, when there is no rain. A mulch will slow water evaporation from the soil.

To save time, money and water you may wish to install an irrigation system. Irrigation systems apply the water exactly where it is needed, near the roots, and reduce the amount of water lost to evaporation. They can be very complex or very simple depending on your needs. A simple irrigation system would involve laying soaker hoses around your garden beds under the mulch. Consult with your local garden centres or landscape professionals for more information.

Annuals in hanging baskets and planters will need to be watered more frequently than plants in the ground. The smaller the container, the more often the plants will need watering. Containers and hanging moss baskets may need to be watered twice daily during hot, sunny weather.

Fertilizing

Your local garden centre should carry a good supply of both organic and chemical fertilizers. Always follow the directions carefully because using too much fertilizer can kill your plants by burning their roots. Whenever possible, use organic fertilizers, which are generally less concentrated and less likely to burn your plants.

Many annuals will flower most profusely if they are fertilized regularly. Some gardeners fertilize hanging baskets and container gardens every time they water, using a very dilute fertilizer so as not to burn the plants. Too much

Pinching off spent flowers

it blooms to encourage side shoots to develop. Some tall annuals, such as larkspur and hollyhocks, require staking with bamboo or other tall, thin stakes. Tie the plant loosely to the stake; strips of nylon hosiery make soft ties that won't cut into the plant. Stake bushy plants with twiggy branches or support rings. Insert the twigs or rings around the plant when it is small and it will grow to fill in and hide the stakes.

If annuals appear tired and withered by mid-summer, try trimming them back to encourage a second blooming. Mounding or low-growing annuals, such as petunias, respond well to trimming. Take your garden shears and trim back one-quarter to one-half of the plant growth. New growth will sprout along with a second flush of flowers.

Deadheading (removing faded flowers) is important in maintaining the health of annuals and in prolonging their bloom. Get into the habit of picking off spent flowers as you are looking around your garden; a little deadheading each day will save you a big job later. Some plants, such as impatiens, are self-cleaning, meaning that they drop their faded blossoms on their own and do not need deadheading.

fertilizer can result in plants that produce weak growth that is susceptible to pest and disease problems. Some plants, such as nasturtiums, grow better without fertilizer and may produce few or no flowers when fertilized excessively.

Fertilizer comes in many forms. Liquids or water-soluble powders are easiest to use when watering. Slow-release pellets or granules are mixed into the garden or potting soil, or sprinkled around the plant and left to work over summer.

Grooming

Good grooming will keep your annuals looking neat, make them flower more profusely and help prevent pest and disease problems. Grooming may include pinching, deadheading, trimming and staking.

Pinch out (remove by hand or with scissors) any straggly growth and the tips of leggy annuals. Plants in cellpacks may have developed straggly growth trying to get light. Pinch back the long growth when planting to encourage bushier growth.

Some tall annuals cannot be pinched. Remove the main shoot after

Growing Perennials as Annuals

Many plants grown as annuals are actually perennials such as geraniums, or shrubs such as fuchsia, which originated in warmer climates and are unable to survive our cold winters. Other plants grown as annuals are biennials, and are started very early in the year to allow them to grow and flower in a single season. These perennials and biennials are listed as such in the individual entries in this book. You can use several techniques to keep these plants for more than one summer.

Some tropical perennials are given special treatment to help them survive winter, or they are simply brought inside and treated as houseplants in the colder months.

A reverse hardening-off process is used to acclimatize plants to an indoor environment. Plants such as geranium and heliotrope, which are grown in the sun all summer, are gradually moved to shady garden spots. This gives them a chance to develop more efficient leaves, capable of surviving in the comparatively limited light indoors.

Impatiens are self-cleaning.

Perennials with tuberous roots can be stored over winter and replanted in late winter or early spring. Dig up plants such as canna, four-o'clock flower in fall after the plant dies back but before the ground freezes. Shake the loose dirt away from the roots and let them dry out a bit in a cool dark place. Once they are dry, the rest of the soil should brush away. Dust the tubers with an anti-fungal powder (found at garden centres) before storing them in moist peat moss or coarse sawdust. Keep them in a dark, dry place that is cold but doesn't freeze. Pot them if they start to sprout, and keep them in a bright window and in moist soil. By late winter or early spring they should be potted up, whether they have already started sprouting or not, to prepare them for spring planting.

Cuttings from angelonia can be grown over the winter for plants in spring.

Cuttings can be taken from large or fast-growing plants such as licorice plant, geraniums and pentas. Grow late-summer cuttings indoors in pots over winter for new spring plants.

If winter storage sounds like too much work, replace your annuals each year and leave the hard work to the growers.

Canna rhizomes can be dug up and stored indoors over winter.

Problems & Pests

New annuals are planted each spring, and often different species are grown each year. These factors make it difficult for pests and diseases to find their preferred host plants and establish a population. However, because annual species are often grown together in masses, any problems that do set in over summer are likely to attack all the plants.

For many years, pest control meant spraying or dusting, with the goal to eliminate every pest in the landscape. A more moderate approach advocated today is IPM (Integrated Pest Management or Integrated Plant Management). The goal of IPM is to reduce pest problems to levels at which only negligible damage is done. Of course, you must determine what degree of damage is acceptable to you. Consider whether a pest's damage is localized or covers the entire plant. Will the damage kill the plant, or is it affecting only the outward appearance? Are there methods of controlling the pest without chemicals?

Chemicals should be used only as a last resort. They can endanger the gardener and his or her family and pets, and they kill good organisms along with bad, leaving the garden vulnerable to even worse attacks. A good IPM program includes learning about your plants and the conditions they need for healthy growth, what pests might affect your plants, where and when to look for those pests and how to control them. Keep records of pest damage because your observations can reveal patterns useful in spotting recurring problems and in planning your maintenance regime.

A responsible pest-management program has four steps. Cultural controls are the most important. Physical controls should be attempted next, followed by biological controls. Use chemical controls only when the other possibilities have been exhausted.

Cultural controls are the gardening techniques you use daily. Keeping your plants as healthy as possible is the best defence against pests. Growing annuals in the conditions they prefer and keeping your soil healthy, with plenty of organic matter, are just two of the cultural controls you can use to manage pests. Choose varieties of annuals that are resistant to problems. Space the plants so that they have good air circulation around them and are not stressed from competing for light, nutrients and space. Remove plants from the landscape if they are decimated by the same pests every year. Remove and burn or take to a permitted dump site diseased foliage and branches. Prevent the spread of disease by keeping your gardening tools clean and by tidying up fallen leaves and dead plant matter at the end of every growing season.

Physical controls are generally used to combat insect problems. An example of such a control is picking insects off plants by hand, which is not that daunting if you catch the problem when it is just beginning. Large, slow insects are particularly easy to pick off. Other physical controls include barriers that stop insects from getting to the plant, and traps that catch or confuse insects. Physical control of diseases often necessitates removing the infected part or parts of the plant to prevent the spread of the problem.

Biological controls make use of populations of natural predators. Such animals as birds, snakes, frogs, spiders, lady beetles and certain bacteria help keep pest populations at a manageable

Ground beetles are effective insect predators.

level. Encourage these creatures to take up permanent residence in your garden. A birdbath and birdfeeder will encourage birds to enjoy your yard and feed on a wide variety of insect pests. Many beneficial insects are probably already living in your landscape, and you can encourage them to stay by planting appropriate food sources. Many beneficial insects eat nectar from flowers such as the perennial yarrow.

Chemical controls should rarely be necessary, but if you must use them there should be some organic options available at garden centres. Organic sprays are no less dangerous than chemical ones, but they will break down into harmless compounds. The main drawback to using any chemicals is that they may also kill the beneficial insects you have been trying to attract to your garden. Follow the manufacturer's instructions carefully. A large amount of insecticide is not going to be any more effective in controlling pests than the recommended amount. Note that if a particular pest is not listed on the package, it will not be controlled by that product. Proper and early identification of pests is vital to finding a quick solution.

While cultural, physical, biological and chemical controls are all possible defences against insects, diseases can be controlled only culturally. Weakened plants succumb to diseases more readily than healthy plants, although some diseases can infect plants regardless of their level of health. Prevention is often the only hope: once a plant has been infected, it should probably be destroyed in order to prevent the disease from spreading.

GLOSSARY OF PESTS & DISEASES

ANTHRACNOSE
Fungus. Yellow or brown spots on leaves; sunken lesions and blisters on stems; can kill plant.

What to Do: Choose resistant varieties and cultivars; keep soil well drained; thin out stems to improve air circulation; avoid handling wet foliage. Remove and destroy infected plant parts; clean up and destroy debris from infected plants at end of growing season.

APHIDS
Ladybird beetle larvae are voracious aphid feeders. Tiny, pear-shaped insects, winged or wingless; green, black, brown, red or grey. Cluster along stems, on buds and on leaves. Suck sap from plants; cause distorted or stunted growth. Sticky honeydew forms on surfaces and encourages sooty mold growth.

What to Do: Squish small colonies by hand; dislodge them with water spray; many predatory insects and birds feed on them; spray serious infestations with insecticidal soap or neem oil.

Aphids

ASTER YELLOWS

Transmitted by leafhoppers. Acts like a virus, causing stunted or deformed growth, yellowed and deformed leaves, dwarfed and greenish flowers; can kill plant.

What to Do: Control leafhoppers with insecticidal soap; remove and destroy infected plants; destroy any local weeds sharing the symptoms. Disease cannot be cured.

BEETLES

Many types and sizes; usually round with hard, shell-like outer wings covering membranous inner wings. Some are beneficial, e.g., ladybird beetles ('ladybugs'); others, e.g., June beetles, eat plants. Larvae: see Borers, Grubs. Leave wide range of chewing damage: make small or large holes in or around margins of leaves; consume entire leaves or areas between leaf veins ('skeletonize'); may also chew holes in flowers.

Japanese beetles are pests in the garden.

What to Do: Pick beetles off at night and drop them into an old coffee can half filled with soapy water (soap prevents them from floating); spread an old sheet under plants and shake off beetles to collect and dispose of them. Spray heavy infestations with neem oil.

BLIGHT

Fungal diseases, many types, e.g., leaf blight, grey mold (Botrytis blight), snow blight. Leaves, stems and flowers blacken, rot and die.

What to Do: Thin stems to improve air circulation; keep mulch away from base of plant; remove debris from garden at end of growing season. Remove and destroy infected plant parts.

BORERS

Larvae of some moths, wasps, beetles; among the most damaging plant pests. Burrow into plant stems, branches, leaves and/or roots; destroy vascular tissue (plant veins and arteries) and structural strength. Worm-like; vary in size and get bigger as they bore through plants. Burrow and weaken stems to cause breakage; leaves will wilt; may see tunnels in leaves, stems or roots; rhizomes may be hollowed out entirely or in part.

What to Do: May be able to squish within leaves. Remove and destroy bored parts; may need to dig up and destroy infected roots and rhizomes.

BUGS

Small insects, up to 1.25 cm ($\frac{1}{2}$") long; green, brown, black or brightly coloured and patterned. Many beneficial; a few pierce plants to suck out sap. Toxins may be injected that deform plants; sunken areas left where pierced; leaves rip as they grow; leaves, buds and new growth may be dwarfed and deformed.

What to Do: Remove debris and weeds from around plants in fall to destroy overwintering sites. Pick off by hand and drop into soapy water; spray plants with insecticidal soap.

Caterpillar eating a flower

CATERPILLARS

Larvae of butterflies, moths, sawflies. Include bagworms, budworms, case bearers, cutworms, leaf rollers, leaf tiers, loopers. Chew foliage and buds; can completely defoliate a plant if infestation severe.

What to Do: Removal from plant is best control. Use a strong spray of water and soap or pick caterpillars off by hand if plant is small enough. Control biologically using the naturally occuring soil bacterium *Bacillus thuringiensis* var. *kurstaki* or *B.t.* for short (commercially available), which breaks down gut lining of caterpillars. Can also use neem oil. Or just leave them alone to transform into butterflies.

CLUBROOT

Soilborne fungus spreads by infected transplants and infested soil on garden tools, shoes. Causes leaves to wilt, turn yellow and drop off; stunts growth of large plants, may kill young ones. Roots of infected plants are swollen, distorted and sometimes rotting. Fungus can survive for many years in soil once established.

What to Do: Use seed rather than bedding plants. Keep soil pH high with regular applications of lime. Ensure soil is well-drained and weed free. Keep garden tools and footwear clean. Destroy all parts of infected plants (do not compost), and do not plant any cabbage family plants in infected soil for 5-7 years.

GALLS

Unusual swellings of plant tissues. Can affect leaves, buds, stems, flowers, fruit. May be caused by insects or diseases. Often a gall affects a single genus or species.

What to Do: Cut galls out of plant and destroy them. Galls caused by insects usually contain the insect's eggs and juvenile forms. Prevent these galls by controlling insect before it lays eggs; otherwise try to remove and destroy infected tissue before the young insects emerge. Generally insect galls are more unsightly than damaging to plants. Galls caused by diseases often require destruction of plant. Avoid placing other plants susceptible to same disease in that location.

GREY MOLD

see Blight

GRUBS

Larvae of different beetles, commonly found below soil level; usually curled in C-shape. Body white or grey; head may be white, grey, brown or reddish. Problematic in lawns; may feed on plant roots. Plant wilts despite regular watering; may pull easily out of ground in severe cases.

What to Do: Toss any grubs found while digging onto a stone path or patio for birds to devour; apply parasitic nematodes or milky disease spore to infested soil (ask at your local garden centre).

LEAFHOPPERS

Small, wedge-shaped insects; can be green, brown, grey or multi-coloured.

Jump around frantically when disturbed. Suck juice from plant leaves. Cause distorted growth. Carry diseases such as aster yellows.

What to Do: Encourage predators by planting nectar-producing species like yarrow. Wash insects off with strong spray of water; spray with insecticidal soap or neem oil.

Leaf miner damage

LEAF MINERS

Tiny, stubby larvae of some butterflies and moths; may be yellow or green. Tunnel within leaves leaving winding trails; tunneled areas lighter in colour than rest of leaf. Unsightly rather than health risk to plant.

What to Do: : Remove debris from area in fall to destroy overwintering sites; attract parasitic wasps with nectar plants such as yarrow. Remove and destroy infected foliage; can sometimes squish by hand within leaf.

LEAF SPOT

Two common types. Bacterial: small speckled spots grow to encompass entire leaves; brown or purple in colour; leaves may drop. Fungal: black, brown or yellow spots; leaves wither.

What to Do: Bacterial infection more severe; must remove entire plant. For fungal infection, remove and destroy infected plant parts. Sterilize removal

tools; avoid wetting foliage or touching wet foliage; remove and destroy debris at end of growing season. Spray plant with neem oil for fungal infection.

MEALYBUGS

Tiny crawling insects related to aphids; appear to be covered with white fuzz or flour. Sucking damage stunts and stresses plant. Mealybugs excrete honeydew that promotes growth of sooty mold.

What to Do: Remove by hand on smaller plants; wash plant off with soap and water; wipe off with alcohol-soaked swabs; remove leaves with heavy infestations; encourage or introduce natural predators such as mealybug destroyer beetle and parasitic wasps; spray with insecticidal soap or neem oil. Keep in mind larvae of mealybug destroyer beetles look like very large mealybugs.

Powdery mildew

MILDEW

Two types, both caused by fungus, but with slightly different symptoms. *Downy mildew:* yellow spots on upper sides of leaves and downy fuzz on undersides; fuzz may be yellow, white or grey. *Powdery mildew:* white or grey powdery coating on leaf surfaces, doesn't brush off.

What to Do: Choose resistant cultivars; space plants well; thin stems to encourage air circulation; tidy any debris in fall. Remove and destroy infected leaves or other parts. Spray with neem oil.

MITES

Tiny, eight-legged relatives of spiders. Almost invisible to naked eye; red, yellow or green; usually found on undersides of plant leaves. May see fine webbing on leaves and stems; may see mites moving on leaf undersides; leaves become discoloured and speckled, then turn brown and shrivel up.

What to Do: Wash off with strong spray of water daily until all signs of infestation are gone; predatory mites available through garden centres; spray plants with insecticidal soap or neem oil.

MOSAIC

see Viruses

NEMATODES

Tiny worms that give plants disease symptoms. One type infects foliage and stems; the other infects roots. *Foliar:* yellow spots that turn brown on leaves; leaves shrivel and wither; problem starts on lowest leaves and works up plant. *Root-knot:* plant is stunted; may wilt; yellow spots on leaves; roots have tiny bumps or knots.

What to Do: Mulch soil, add organic matter, clean up debris in fall. Don't touch wet foliage of infected plants; can add parasitic nematodes to soil. Remove infected plants in extreme cases.

ROT

Several different fungi that affect different parts of the plant and can kill plant. *Crown rot* (stem rot): affects base of plant, causing stems to blacken and fall over and leaves to yellow and wilt.

Root rot: leaves yellow and plant wilts; digging up plant will show roots rotted away.

What to Do: Keep soil well drained; don't damage plant if you are digging around it; keep mulches away from plant base. Destroy infected plant if whole plant affected.

RUST

Fungi. Pale spots on upper leaf surfaces; orange, fuzzy or dusty spots on leaf undersides.

What to Do: Choose rust-resistant varieties and cultivars; avoid handling wet leaves; provide plant with good air circulation; clear up garden debris at end of season. Remove and destroy infected plant parts. Spray with neem oil.

SCALE INSECTS

Tiny, shelled insects that suck sap, weakening and possibly killing plant or making it vulnerable to other problems. Once female scale insect has pierced plant with mouthpart, it is there for life. Juvenile scale insects are called crawlers.

What to Do: Wipe off with alcohol-soaked swabs; spray with water to dislodge crawlers; encourage natural predators and parasites; dispose of infected material carefully at end of summer.

SLUGS & SNAILS

Both mollusks; slugs lack shells, snails have spiral shells. Up to 20cm (8") long, many smaller. Slimy, smooth skin; grey, green, black, beige, yellow or spotted. Leave large, ragged holes in leaves and silvery slime trails on and around plants.

What to Do: Attach strips of copper to wood around raised beds or to smaller boards inserted around

Slug on leaf

susceptible groups of plants; slugs and snails get shocked if they touch copper surfaces. Pick off by hand in the evening and squish with boot or drop in can of soapy water. Spread wood ash or diatomaceous earth (available in garden centres) on ground around plants; it will pierce their soft bodies and cause them to dehydrate. Do not use diatomaceous earth intended for swimming pool filters. Slug baits containing iron phosphate are not harmful to humans or animals and control slugs very well when used according to package directions. If slugs damaged garden last season, begin controls as soon as new green shoots appear in spring.

SMUT

Fungus. May cause galls or streaking on leaves.

What to Do: Treat as for rust.

SOOTY MOLD

Fungus. Thin black film forms on leaf surfaces and reduces amount of light getting to leaves.

What to Do: Wipe mold off leaf surfaces; control insects such as aphids, mealybugs, whiteflies (honeydew left on leaves encourages mold).

THRIPS

Difficult to see; may be visible if you disturb them by blowing gently on an infested flower. Yellow, black or brown; tiny, slender, with narrow fringed

wings. Suck juice out of plant cells, particularly in flowers and buds, causing mottled petals and leaves, dying buds and distorted and stunted growth.

What to Do: Remove and destroy infected plant parts; encourage native predatory insects with nectar plants like yarrow; spray severe infestations with insecticidal soap or neem oil.

VIRUSES

Plant may be stunted and leaves and flowers distorted, streaked or discoloured. Example: tobacco mosaic virus.

What to Do: Viral diseases in plants cannot be controlled. Destroy infected plants; disinfect tools that have been used on virus-infected plants; control insects like aphids, leafhoppers and whiteflies that spread disease.

Mosaic virus damage

WHITEFLIES

Flying insects that flutter up into the air when the plant is disturbed. Tiny, moth-like, white; live on undersides of plant leaves. Suck juice out of plant leaves, causing yellowed leaves and weakened plants; leave sticky honeydew on leaves, encouraging sooty mold growth.

What to Do: Destroy weeds where insects may live. Attract native predatory beetles and parasitic wasps with nectar plants like yarrow; spray severe cases with insecticidal soap. Can make a sticky flypaper-like trap by mounting tin can on stake; wrap can with yellow paper and cover with clear plastic bag smeared with petroleum jelly; replace bag when full of flies.

WILT

If watering hasn't helped a wilted plant, one of two wilt fungi may be at fault. *Fusarium wilt:* plant wilts, leaves turn yellow then die; symptoms generally appear first on one part of plant before spreading to other parts. *Verti-*

cillium wilt: plant wilts; leaves curl up at edges; leaves turn yellow then drop off; plant may die.

What to Do: Both wilts are difficult to control. Choose resistant plant varieties and cultivars; clean up debris at end of growing season. Destroy infected plants; solarize (sterilize) soil before replanting (this may help if you've lost an entire bed of plants to these fungi)—contact local garden centre for assistance.

WORMS

see Caterpillars, Nematodes

PEST CONTROL ALTERNATIVES

The following treatments for pests and diseases allow the gardener some measure of control without resorting to harmful chemical fungicides and pesticides.

ANT CONTROL

Mix 700 ml (3 c.) water, 250 ml (1 c.) white sugar and 20 ml (4 tsp.) liquid boric acid in a pot. Bring this mix just to a boil and remove it from the heat source. Let the mix cool. Pour small amounts of the cooled mix into bottlecaps or other very small containers and place them around the ant-infested area. You can also try setting out a mixture of equal parts powdered borax and icing sugar (no water).

ANTI-TRANSPIRANTS

These products were developed to reduce water transpiration, or loss of water, in plants. The waxy polymers surround fungal spores, preventing the spread of spores to nearby leaves and stems. When applied according to label directions, these products are environmentally friendly. Available from garden centres.

BAKING SODA & CITRUS OIL

This mixture treats both leaf spot and powdery mildew. In a spray bottle, mix 20 ml (4 tsp.) baking soda, 15 ml (1 tbsp.) citrus oil and 4 l (1 gal.) water. Spray the foliage lightly, including the undersides. Do not pour or spray this mix directly onto soil.

BAKING SODA & HORTICULTURAL OIL

Research has confirmed the effectiveness of this mixture against powdery mildew. Mix 20 ml (4 tsp.) baking soda, 15 ml (1 tbsp.) horticultural oil in 4 l (1 gal.) water. Fill a spray bottle and spray the foliage lightly, including the undersides. Do not pour or spray this mix directly onto soil.

COFFEE GROUNDS SPRAY

Boil 1 kg (2 lb.) used coffee grounds in 11 l (3 gal.) water for about 10 minutes.

Allow to cool; strain the grounds out. Apply as a spray to reduce problems with whiteflies.

COMPOST TEA

Mix 500 g–1 kg (1–2 lb.) compost in 19 l (5 gal.) of water. Let sit for four to seven days. Dilute the mix until it resembles weak tea. Use during normal watering or apply as a foliar spray to prevent or treat fungal diseases.

FISH EMULSION/SEAWEED (KELP)

These products are usually used as foliar nutrient feeds but appear to also work against fungal diseases, either by preventing the fungus from spreading to noninfected areas or by changing the growing conditions for the fungus.

GARLIC SPRAY

This spray is an effective, organic means of controlling aphids, leafhoppers, whiteflies and some fungi and nematodes. Soak 90 ml (6 tbsp.) finely minced garlic in 10 ml (2 tsp.) mineral oil for at least 24 hours. Add 0.5 l (1 pt.) of water and 7.5 ml (1½ tsp.) of

liquid dish soap. Stir and strain into a glass container for storage. Combine 15–30 ml (1–2 tbsp.) of this concentrate with 0.5 l (2 c.) water to make a spray. Test the spray on a couple of leaves and check after two days for any damage. If no damage, spray infested plants thoroughly, ensuring good coverage of the foliage.

HORTICULTURAL OIL

Mix 75 ml (5 tbsp.) horticultural oil per 4 l (1 gal.) of water and apply as a spray for a variety of insect and fungal problems.

INSECTICIDAL SOAP

Mix 5 ml (1 tsp.) of mild dish detergent or pure soap (biodegradable options are available) with 1 l (1 qt.) of water in a clean spray bottle. Spray the surfaces of insect-infested plants and rinse well within an hour of spraying to avoid foliage discolouring.

NEEM OIL

Neem oil is derived from the neem tree (native to India) and is used as an insecticide, miticide and fungicide. Most effective when used preventively. Apply when conditions are favourable for disease development. Neem is virtually harmless to most beneficial insects and microorganisms.

SULFUR AND LIME-SULFUR

These products are good as preventive measures for fungal diseases. You can purchase ready-made products or wettable powders that you mix yourself. Do not spray when the temperature is expected to be 32° C (90° F) or higher, or you may damage your plants.

About This Guide

The annuals in this book are organized alphabetically by their most familiar, local common names. Other common names and scientific names appear after the primary reference, and all names can be found in the index. The illustrated Flowers at a Glance section at the beginning of the book will familiarize you with the different flowers quickly, and it will help you find a plant if you aren't sure what it's called.

Clearly indicated at the beginning of each entry are height and spread ranges and flower colours. At the back of the book, you will find a Quick Reference Chart that summarizes different features and requirements of the annuals; you will find this chart handy when planning diversity in your garden.

Each entry gives clear instructions and tips for seeding, planting and growing the annual, and it recommends many of our favourite species and varieties. Note: If height and spread ranges are not indicated for a recommended plant, assume these values are the same as the ranges at the beginning of the entry. Keep in mind, too, that many more hybrids, cultivars and varieties are often available. Check with your local greenhouses or garden centres when making your selection.

Pests or diseases that commonly afflict a plant, if any, are also listed for each entry. Consult the 'Problems & Pests' section of the introduction for information on how to solve these problems.

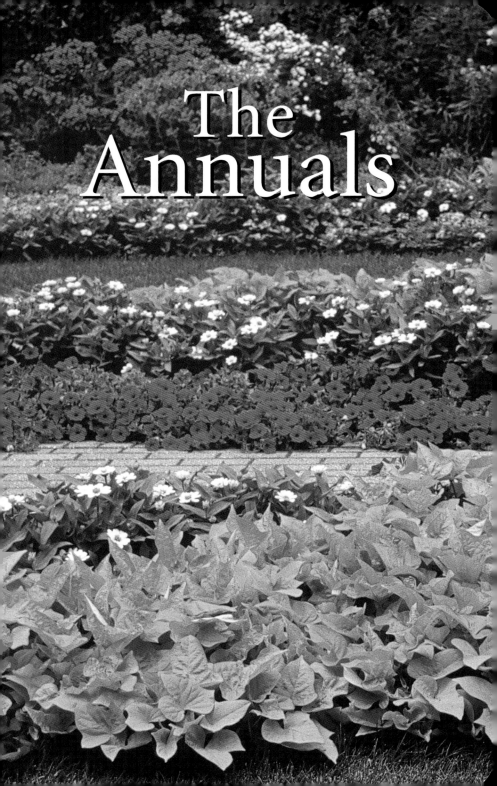

The
Annuals

African Daisy

Dimorphotheca

Height: 30–45 cm (12–18") **Spread:** 30 cm (12") **Flower colour:** white, orange, yellow, red, pink; often with brown, yellow, black, orange or purple centres

VILLAGES ON THE FRENCH RIVIERA, SUCH AS EZE, EXPERIENCE year-round warmth. I had the opportunity to tour the lush, tropical gardens of this region years ago. Bananas, dates, carob trees and lemon and orange trees are quite common there, a testament to their love of the tropical environment. African daisies grow throughout the region, mostly in rock gardens and trailing down steep rock embankments, petals gleaming in the sun. I've also grown African daisies next to a brick wall in my garden here in Alberta. It's easy to be fooled by their dainty appearance, but they are tough little plants that seem to thrive on drought to some extent and love the conditions that the prairies have to offer just as much as they love southern France.

Planting

Seeding: Indoors in early spring; direct sow after last frost

Planting out: After last frost

Spacing: 30 cm (12")

Growing

African daisies like **full sun**. The soil should be **light, fertile** and **well drained**. These plants are drought resistant.

If growing this flower from seed, water young seedlings freely. Otherwise they will fail to thrive.

African daisies do not grow well in rainy weather. Plant them under the eaves of the house, in window boxes or in raised beds to protect them from too much rain.

Tips

African daisies are most attractive when planted in groups or masses. Use these flowers in beds and borders. The flowers close at night and on cloudy days, so although they can be cut for flower arrangements, they might close if the vase isn't getting enough light.

Recommended

D. pluvialis (cape marigold, rain daisy, African daisy) has white flowers with purple on the undersides and bases of the petals. **'Glistening White'** is a compact plant that bears large, pure white flowers with black centres.

D. 'Salmon Queen' bears salmon and apricot pink flowers on plants that spread to about 45 cm (18").

D. sinuata (star of the veldt) forms a 30–45 cm (12–18") mound. It bears yellow, orange, white or pink daisy-like flowers all summer. Cultivars with larger flowers are available.

D. 'Starshine' is a low, mound-forming cultivar with shiny flowers in pink, orange, white or red, with yellow centres.

D. pluvialis (above), *D. sinuata* (below)

Problems & Pests

Fungal problems are likely to occur in hot and wet locations. Dry, cool places produce healthy plants that are less susceptible to disease.

Ageratum
Floss Flower
Ageratum

Height: 15–90 cm (6–36") **Spread:** 15–45 cm (6–18") **Flower colour:** white, pink, mauve, blue

AGERATUM IS NOT ONLY A PRETTY LITTLE FLOWERING ANNUAL, but it is also often grown to attract more bees and other pollinators into your garden. Ageratum has been part of the prairie landscape for generations and has rarely moved out of the spotlight. The small, fluffy flowers are beautiful in little vases mixed with pansies. This combination is also adorable in the garden, the contrasting flowerheads complementing one another nicely. Try planting the shorter varieties of ageratum in rock gardens and the taller varieties in containers and mixed beds. If using ageratum for edging, you will find each plant grows uniformly and bears flowers all summer long.

Planting

Seeding: Indoors in early spring; direct sow after last frost. Don't cover the seeds; they need light to germinate.

Planting out: Once soil has warmed

Spacing: 10–30 cm (4–12")

Growing

Ageratum prefers **full sun** but tolerates partial shade. The soil should be **fertile, moist** and **well drained**. This plant doesn't like to have its soil dry out; a moisture-retaining mulch will reduce the need to water too frequently. Don't mulch too thickly or too close to the base of the plant or it may develop crown rot or root rot.

Though this plant needs deadheading to keep it flowering, the blossoms are extraordinarily long-lived, making ageratum an easy-care plant for sunny gardens.

A. houstonianum cultivar (above)
A. houstonianum (below)

To dry ageratum flowers for crafts and floral arrangements, cut fresh flowers in the morning, bundle them together with rubber bands and hang them upside down in a location with good air circulation.

Tips

The smaller varieties, which become almost completely covered with fluffy flowerheads, make excellent edging plants for flowerbeds. They are also attractive grouped in masses or grown in pots. The taller varieties are useful in the centre of a flowerbed and make interesting cut flowers.

The original species is a tall, leggy plant that was not considered attractive enough for the annual border but was used in the cutting garden. New cultivars are much more compact, and ageratum is now a proudly displayed annual.

The specific epithet houstanianum *refers not to the Texas city but to William Houston, who collected the flowers in Mexico and the Antilles.*

'Blue Hawaii' (photos this page)

Recommended

A. houstonianum forms a large, leggy mound that can grow up to 60 cm (24") tall. Clusters of fuzzy blue, white or pink flowers are held above the foliage. Many cultivars are available; most have been developed to maintain a low, compact form that is more useful in the border. **Artist Hybrids** are vigorous performers producing flowers in shades of true blue and purple-pink in 20–30 cm (8–12") heights, including a larger-leafed, upright hybrid that grows to 30–45 cm (12–18") in height. **'Bavaria'** grows about 25 cm (10") tall with blue and white bicoloured flowers. **'Blue Hawaii'** is a compact plant 15–20 cm (6–8") tall, with blue flowers. **'Blue Horizon'** is an upright cultivar with lavender blue flowers. It grows 60–90 cm (24–36") tall. **'Pinky Improved'** is a compact plant with subtle, dusky pink flowers. **'Red Sea'** bears deep pinky red flowers while **'Summer Snow'** has white flowers.

'Blue Hawaii' (above), 'Blue Horizon' (below)

Problems & Pests

Powdery mildew may become a problem. Be sure to plant ageratum in a location with good air circulation to help prevent fungal diseases.

The genus name Ageratum *is derived from a Greek word meaning "without age," a reference to the long-lasting flowers.*

Amaranth

Amaranthus

Height: 91 cm–1.5 m (3–5') **Spread:** 30–75 cm (12–30") **Flower colour:** red, yellow, green; flowers inconspicuous in some species grown for foliage

OVER THE YEARS, NEW AND EXCITING AMARANTH CULTIVARS have been created and made available to prairie gardeners. Each is unique and fascinating in its own right, bearing elegant, colourful spikes and tassel-like clusters of flowers that offer show-stopping quality. I like to plant varieties of amaranth in large, dramatic containers. They're ideal for this application because they can tolerate being left to dry out a little when the days grow hotter and the soil dries out faster. Bugs aren't all that interested in amaranth and will leave them alone, and diseases aren't a problem, either. You can relax and enjoy yourself with amaranth in your garden.

Planting

Seeding: Indoors about three weeks before last frost; direct sow once soil has warmed

Planting out: Once soil has warmed

Spacing: 30–61 cm (12–24")

Growing

A location in **full sun** is preferable. The soil should be **poor to average** and **well drained**. Don't give these plants rich soil or overfertilize them, or their growth will be tall, soft and prone to falling over. Joseph's coat will also lose some of its leaf colour if overfertilized; its colours will be more brilliant in poor soil.

Seeds started indoors should be planted in peat pots or pellets to avoid disturbing the roots when transplanting them.

Love-lies-bleeding self-seeds and can show up year after year. Unwanted plants are easy to uproot when they are young.

A. caudatus 'Viridis' (above)
A. cruentus cultivar (below)

Amaranth has astringent properties and has been used by herbalists to stop bleeding and to treat diarrhea.

A. tricolor 'Illumination' (above)

A. caudatus (centre), A. tricolor (below), A. caudatus (opposite page)

Tips

Love-lies-bleeding is attractive grouped in borders or in mixed containers, where it requires very little care or water. Joseph's coat is a bright, striking plant that is best used as an annual specimen plant in a small group rather than in a large mass planting, where it quickly becomes overwhelming. It is also attractive mixed with large foliage plants in the back of a border.

Recommended

A. caudatus (love-lies-bleeding, tassel flower, velvet flower) has long, drooping, rope-like, fluffy red, yellow or green flower spikes that can be air dried. The plant has erect stems and grows 91 cm–1.5 m (3–5') tall and 45–75 cm (18–30") wide. **'Love-Lies-Bleeding'** bears dark red tassels of flowers. **Magic Fountains Mix** ranges in height from 50 cm (20") to 1.2 m (4'). The flowerheads are borne in shades of red, gold, green

and burgundy, both in cascading and upright forms. **'Viridis'** bears tassels of light green flowers.

A. cruentus (*A. paniculatus*; purple amaranth, red amaranth, prince's feather) is an upright species that grows up to 1.8 m (6') tall and 45 cm (18") wide. It produces purplish green leaves and greenish red, pendent flowers followed by red-brown, purple or yellow seedheads. Often the cultivars are more popular and available than the species. **'Golden Giant'** has prominent golden seedheads and **'Marvel Bronze,'** a shorter cultivar growing 91 cm–1.2 m (3–4'), produces dark purple-bronze foliage and deep burgundy red, upright flower plumes.

A. tricolor (Chinese spinach, Joseph's coat) is a bushy, upright plant that grows up to 91 cm–1.2 m (3–4') tall and 30–61 cm (12–24") wide. The brightly coloured foliage is variegated and can be green, red, bronze, chocolatey purple, orange, yellow or gold. The flowers of the species and its cultivars are inconspicuous. **'Aurora's'** newest growth is bright yellow, contrasting with the dark green foliage at the base of each stem. It grows 30–45 cm (12–18") tall. The cultivar **'Illumination'** has hanging foliage in crimson and gold. It grows 1.2 m (4') tall and 30 cm (12") wide. **'Joseph's Coat'** has green, yellow and bronze lower leaves and red and gold new leaves.

Problems & Pests

Cold nights below 10° C (50° F) will cause leaf drop. Rust, leaf spot, root rot, aphids and some viral diseases are potential problems.

Angelonia

Angelonia

Height: 30–60 cm (12–24") **Spread:** 30 cm (12") **Flower colour:** purple, blue, white, pink

ANGELONIA BROKE INTO THE MARKET a few years ago. It has left an indelible mark and is likely to become a prairie bedding staple. Planted in a pot, or nestled among other annuals and perennials in a garden bed, this plant will not let you down. It is content in just about any circumstance and is one annual that more gardeners should consider trying, if they're looking to grow something different and new. Angelonia has great staying power, rarely needs staking and is the ideal substitute for most taller flowering annuals grown in containers, including salvias, snapdragons and stocks.

The individual flowers look a bit like orchid blossoms, but Angelonia *is actually in the same family as snapdragons.*

Planting

Seeding: Not recommended

Planting out: In warm soil after last frost

Spacing: 20–30 cm (8–12")

Growing

Angelonia prefers **full sun** but tolerates a bit of shade. The soil should be **fertile, moist** and **well drained**. Though this plant grows naturally in damp areas, such as along ditches and near ponds, it is fairly drought tolerant.

This tender subshrub is not worth trying to save from year to year because it tends to lose its attractive habit as it matures. Cuttings can be taken in late summer and grown indoors over the winter to be used the following summer.

Tips

With its loose, airy spikes of orchid-like flowers, angelonia makes a welcome addition to the annual or mixed border. Include it in a pond-side or streamside planting or in a mixed planter.

Recommended

A. angustifolia is a perennial that is treated as an annual. It is a bushy, upright plant with loose spikes of flowers in varied shades of purple. **'Alba'** bears white flowers. **Angelface Hybrids** are available with violet, blue, white or bicoloured flowers. **Angelmist Hybrids** are available in lavender-pink, white, light pink, deep plum, lavender, purple and purple stripe. **'Blue Pacific'** bears bicoloured flowers of white and violet blue.

'Alba' (above), 'Blue Pacific' (below)

Problems & Pests

Aphids and powdery mildew can cause trouble.

Asarina
Twining Snapdragon
Asarina (Maurandya)

Height: 45 cm–1.8 m (18"–6') **Spread:** equal to height, as trained
Flower colour: purple, pink, blue, white, red; attractive foliage

THIS RELATIVE NEWCOMER IS RELATED TO THE SNAPDRAGON BUT lacks the hinged part of the flower that allows the dragon's mouth to be opened. Asarina is often sold in hanging baskets because of its trailing, bushy growth habit and prolific blooming. It's also a charming addition to a bird garden. Hummingbirds are attracted to bright colours and these fall perfectly into that category. I once saw it grown in an antique mailbox, trailing out of the mail slot and blooming with everything it had. The flowers were violet purple and perched atop the twining foliage, like an invitation to all of the hummingbirds in the neighbourhood, and it worked like a charm.

Planting

Seeding: Direct sow in warm soil; start indoors in early spring

Planting out: After danger of frost has passed

Spacing: 60 cm (24")

Growing

Asarina grows well in **full sun, partial shade** or **light shade**. The soil should be **average to fertile, moist** and **well drained**. The leaves may scorch in hot afternoon sun. These climbers need a trellis or other frame to twine their tendrils around as they climb.

Tips

Asarina can be grown up a trellis or other structure. They look great in containers, where they can trail over the edge or grow up a wire frame. They can also be planted in a border where they will trail along the ground and over any objects they encounter.

Recommended

A. purpusii (*M. purpusii*) is an attractive climbing plant. It grows 45–60 cm (18–24") tall and bears purple, pink or white flowers. **'Victoria Falls'** is a trailing cultivar that bears many flowers in dark pink and is useful in hanging baskets.

A. scandens (*A. erubescens*) is a vigorous climber that flowers quickly from seed and continues to flower until the first hard frost. It grows up to 1.8 m (6') tall, or taller. It bears pink,

A. scandens

white, red, purple or blue flowers. **Jewel Mix** bears flowers in a variety of colours. **'Joan Lorraine'** has purple flowers with white throats.

Problems & Pests

Asarina rarely suffer from any problems.

Asarina is also known and sometimes sold as climbing snapdragon.

Baby's Breath
Gypsophila

Height: 30–90 cm (12–36") **Spread:** 30–60 cm (12–24")
Flower colour: white, pink, mauve

INTRODUCED TO THE HOME GARDEN IN THE 19TH CENTURY, baby's breath was an old-fashioned Victorian filler plant used in mixed flowerbeds and containers. This plant is ornamental not only in the garden, but in fresh or dry arrangements as well. Florist shops always have plenty of the perennial baby's breath on hand for floral arrangements, so the professionals know its value. The taller annual varieties are equally as sought after for arrangements, especially for tussy mussies (small bouquets carried in hand-held metal vases) and small bouquets. Baby's breath will fill in areas with poor alkaline soil, look airy against rock walls and dry well for use in dried floral arrangements and wreaths. The effect of a plant in full bloom is tremendous—it looks like a giant, weightless cloud in the early-summer garden.

Planting

Seeding: Indoors in late winter; direct sow from mid-spring to early summer

Planting out: Mid-spring

Spacing: 20–45 cm (8–18")

Growing

Baby's breath grows best in **full sun**. The soil should be of **poor fertility**, and it should be **light, sandy** and **alkaline**. This plant is drought tolerant; take care not to overwater because it does not grow well in wet soil. Don't space the seedlings too far apart because slightly crowded plants flower more profusely. Individual plants are short-lived, so sow seeds every week or two until early summer to encourage a longer blooming period.

Tips

The clouds of flowers are ideal for rock gardens, rock walls, mixed containers or borders with bold-coloured flowers. Native to the northeastern Mediterranean, baby's breath looks very good in a Mediterranean-style garden.

Recommended

G. elegans forms an upright mound of airy stems, foliage and flowers. The plant grows 30–60 cm (12–24") tall. The flowers are usually white but may have pink or purple veining that gives the flowers a coloured tinge. **'Carminea'** has deep carmine rose flowers. **'Covent Garden'** has very large, white flowers and grows to 50–90 cm (20–36") tall. **'Red Cloud'** has carmine to pink flowers. **'Rosea'** produces pale rose pink flowers.

G. elegans cultivar (above), *G. elegans* (below)

G. muralis grows 30–45 cm (12–18") tall and 30–50 cm (12–20") wide and has dense, dark green foliage and flower clusters held above the foliage. **'Garden Bride'** grows 30 cm (12") tall and bears double or semi-double pink flowers. **'Gypsy,'** a 1997 All-America Selections winner, grows 30–35 cm (12–14") tall and bears semi-double to double pink flowers.

Problems & Pests

Most of the more common problems are fungal diseases that can be prevented by not overwatering and not handling plants when they are wet. Leafhoppers can infect plants with aster yellows.

Bachelor's Buttons
Cornflower, Blue-Bottle
Centaurea

Height: 30 cm –1 m (12–39") **Spread:** 15–60 cm (6–24")
Flower colour: blue, red, pink, white, violet

WHEN PEOPLE HEAR THE WORDS 'CORNFLOWER BLUE,' THEY often are reminded of this flower in a traditional cottage garden setting. This annual has a long history that's been passed from one generation to the next because the seeds are easy to save and pass along. It is hard to find this shade of blue in other flowers, and the violet blue offers a unique contrast to other flower shapes and colours. Although the flowers are edible and can be used to accent special dishes, lending a sweet clove-like flavour, they are not fragrant. Pollinating insects also love this traditional annual. Bees, in particular, love to get their little bodies in between the stamens and hunt for pollen on a hot summer day.

Planting

Seeding: Direct sow in mid-spring or start indoors in late winter

Planting out: Around last frost

Spacing: 30 cm (12") apart

The genus name, Centaurea, *comes from* Kentaurus, *or "centaur," because the mythical centaurs were said to nibble on bachelor's button to restore their vigour.*

Growing

Bachelor's buttons will do best in **full sun. Fertile, moist, well-drained** soil is preferable, but any soil is tolerated. Light frost won't harm the plants.

Seed started indoors should be planted in peat pots or pellets to avoid disturbing roots during transplanting. Shear spent flowers and old foliage in mid-summer for fresh new growth. Deadheading prolongs blooming.

Tips

Bachelor's buttons is a great filler plant in a mixed border, wildflower or cottage-style garden. It is attractive when used in masses or small groups. Grow bachelor's buttons mixed with other plants—as the bachelor's buttons fade, the other plants can fill in the space they leave.

Recommended

C. cyanus is an upright annual that grows 30–90 cm (12–36") tall and spreads 15–60 cm (6–24"). The flowers of this plant are most often

C. cyanus (photos this page)

blue but can be shades of red, pink, violet or white. Plants in the **Boy Series** grow up to 1 m (39") tall and have large, double flowers in many colours. '**Florence**' is a compact, dwarf cultivar that grows 30–45 cm (12–18") tall and has flowers in various colours.

Problems & Pests

Aphids, downy mildew and powdery mildew may cause problems.

Bacopa
Sutera

Height: 7.5–15 cm (3–6") **Spread:** 30–50 cm (12–20")
Flower colour: white, lavender, blue

BACOPA HAS BECOME UNBELIEVABLY POPULAR OVER THE PAST decade, and is highly sought after by prairie gardeners throughout the province. Some become less enamoured after growing it, however, but only because they've grown it in a location in direct sun that is too hot. Bacopa shows its dislike for hot places by flowering less and turning its leaves an unusual bronze colour, especially if allowed to dry out. It works best mixed with other plants, including impatiens and begonias, which share a like of partial shade and moist soil. The most important thing to remember when growing bacopa is to fertilize it on a regular basis, because it is known to be a heavy feeder.

Planting

Seeding: Not recommended

Planting out: Once soil has warmed

Spacing: 30 cm (12")

Growing

Bacopa grows well in **partial shade**, with protection from the hot afternoon sun. The soil should be of **average fertility, humus rich, moist** and **well drained**.

Don't allow this plant to dry out, or the leaves will quickly die. Cutting back dead growth may encourage new shoots to form.

Tips

Bacopa is a popular plant for hanging baskets, mixed containers and window boxes. It is not recommended as a bedding plant because it fizzles quickly when the weather gets hot, particularly if you forget to water. Plant it where you will see it every day and where it will be easy for you to water it.

Recommended

S. cordata, a compact, trailing plant, bears small, white flowers all summer. **'Blue Showers'** bears lavender blue flowers and **'Candy Floss Blue'** has tiny blue flowers. **'Giant Snowflake'** is a vigorous development of 'Snowflake.' **'Gold 'n Pearls'** produces golden variegated foliage and white flowers. **'Lavender Showers'** forms a dense mound of heart-shaped leaves with scalloped edges and tiny, star-shaped flowers on trailing stems. **'Olympic Gold,'** from EuroAmerican, has white flowers and gold-variegated foliage. **'Snowflake,'** one of the first cultivars available, bears white flowers.

'Olympic Gold' (above), *S. cordata* (below)

Problems & Pests

Whiteflies and other small insects can become a real menace to this plant because the dense growth with tiny leaves makes a perfect hiding spot for them.

Bacopa is a perennial that is grown as an annual plant outdoors. It will thrive as a houseplant in a bright room.

Beefsteak Plant

Iresine

Height: 45–60 cm (18–24") **Spread:** 50–60 cm (20–24")
Flower colour: grown for colourful foliage

FORMALLY SOLD STRICTLY AS A HOUSEPLANT, THIS VIBRANT PLANT is one of many "tropicals" that is making its way outdoors for the summer. The striking colour is caused by a pigment that camouflages the green chlorophyll within the leaf. In fact, this plant is also known by many as bloodleaf plant for obvious reasons. The common name also refers to the leaves' resemblance to marbled beef. Beefsteak plant does produce flowers, but they are insignificant at best. Like coleus, this plant is grown for its foliage. In fact, it's best to pinch the flowers out entirely as they emerge because they can actually take away from the look of the brightly veined foliage. There's no end to this annual's use. Even if you're not attracted to the garish foliage, other colour combinations are available in less vivid colour blends.

Planting

Seeding: Not recommended

Planting out: Once soil has warmed and danger of frost has passed

Spacing: 30–45 cm (12–18")

Growing

Beefsteak plant prefers **full to partial sun**, with **some direct sun** to maintain the intense foliar colour. A good **loamy, moist** but **well-drained** soil is best.

Pinch the growing tips out of younger plants to encourage a dense growth. Mature plants should be cut back if they become straggly. The cuttings can be used for propagating.

Beefsteak plants also make fine indoor specimens. Bring them indoors in late summer or fall, prior to a frost and treat them as a houseplant until spring. Cut them back by at least one third and bring them back outdoors for the summer.

Tips

Beefsteak plants are effective when planted in large groupings in mixed beds and borders. They also work well as accent plants in containers. The bright and vivid foliage is striking when planted with chartreuse and yellow variegated plants, including 'Margarita' sweet potato vine, coleus, 'Illumination' vinca and 'Lemon Symphony' osteospermum.

Recommended

I. herbstii (beefsteak plant, chicken gizzard) is an erect, bushy, short-lived perennial that is often grown as an annual. It produces waxy, brightly coloured leaves and stems in bright green, purple, and red

I. herbstii (photos this page)

with contrasting veins. The species grows 60 cm (24") tall and 45 cm (18") wide. **'Aureoreticulata'** has mid-green leaves with bright yellow veins. **'Bloodleaf'** has blood red leaves with brightly contrasting pink veins. **'Brilliantissima'** has rich purple-green leaves and vivid purple veins and **'Wallisii'** is a dwarf cultivar, with dark purple leaves that almost appear black.

Problems & Pests

Aphids and powdery mildew may affect this plant but only rarely.

Bidens

Bidens

Height: 30–45 cm (12–18") **Spread:** 30–45 cm (12–18") or more
Flower colour: yellow

BIDENS IS AN EXCELLENT FILLER PLANT FOR HANGING BASKETS and containers that are calling out for colour and densely growing filler plants. The cheerful yellow blossoms welcome you to explore it more closely. Yellow flowers are always more striking when mixed with purples because they contrast and appear to be brighter and more vibrant than they really are, playing tricks on the gardener's eye. Similar to cosmos and swan river daisies, bidens has finely divided, almost dill-like leaves and a succession of lemon yellow flowers from mid-summer to autumn. With its tolerance to excessive heat, bidens works well in gardens mulched with gravel or tumbling down rock wall embankments, to soften the edges of a common hardscape.

This cheerful plant in the daisy family is always in flower and makes a wonderful annual groundcover.

Planting

Seeding: Direct sow in late spring or start indoors in late winter

Planting out: After last frost

Spacing: 30–45 cm (12–24")

Growing

Bidens grows well in **full sun**. The soil should be **average to fertile, moist** and **well drained**.

If your bidens becomes lank and unruly in summer, shear it back lightly to encourage new growth and fall flowers.

Tips

Bidens can be included in mixed borders, containers, hanging baskets and window boxes. Its fine foliage and attractive flowers make it useful for filling spaces between other plants.

Recommended

B. ferulifolia is a bushy, mounding plant with fine, ferny foliage and bright yellow flowers. The cultivar **'Golden Goddess'** has narrow foliage and larger flowers.

Problems & Pests

Problems can occur with fungal diseases such as leaf spot, powdery mildew and rust.

B. ferulifolia *is native to Arizona and Mexico, so it is well equipped to handle full sun and heat in prairie gardens.*

B. ferulifolia (photos this page)

California Poppy

Eschscholzia

Height: 20–45 cm (8–18") **Spread:** 20–45 cm (8–18") **Flower colour:** orange, yellow, red; less commonly pink, cream; attractive foliage

ONCE, WHEN FLYING INTO THE LOS ANGELES AIRPORT, I SAW thousands of California poppies in bloom on the grass beside the runway, which was striking to say the least. In fact I was surprised to see the colourful flowers in such a location, and I hoped their brilliance wouldn't distract the pilots from landing the plane smoothly. This poppy is such a cheerful addition to the garden, with its shocking and crisp orange or yellow petal colour offset by grey-green leaves. The California State Floral Society liked it so much, they voted to make this poppy their state flower in 1890. California poppies have graced a garden along my driveway for over 12 years. I simply sprinkle the seeds and watch them take off with hardly any effort. They are a joy even when the petals close up in the evening or on cloudy days.

Planting

Seeding: Direct sow in early to mid-spring

Spacing: 15–30 cm (6–12")

Growing

California poppy prefers **full sun**. The soil should be of **poor** or **average fertility** and **well drained**. With too rich a soil, the growth will be lush and green but the plants will bear few, if any, flowers. This plant is drought tolerant once established.

Never start this plant indoors because it dislikes having its roots disturbed. California poppy will sprout quickly when planted directly in the garden. Sow in early spring for blooms in summer.

California poppy requires a lot of water for germination and development of young plants. Until they flower, provide the plants with regular and frequent watering. Once they begin flowering, they are more drought tolerant.

Tips

California poppy can be included in an annual border or annual planting in a cottage garden. This plant self-seeds wherever it is planted; it is perfect for naturalizing in a meadow garden or rock garden where it will come back year after year.

Recommended

E. californica grows 20–45 cm (8–18") tall and wide, forming a mound of delicate, feathery, blue-green foliage. It bears satiny orange or yellow flowers all summer. **'Ballerina'** has a mixture of colours and semi-double or double flowers.

E. californica (photos this page)

'Buttermilk' bears masses of creamy-white, semi-double flowers and blue-green foliage. **'Carmine King'** bears pale apricot, single flowers edged in deep carmine red. **'Chiffon,'** a compact plant up to 20 cm (8") tall, bears semi-double flowers in pink and apricot. **'Mission Bells'** bears ruffled, double and semi-double flowers in mixed and solid shades of orange, yellow, red, cream and pink. **Thai Silk Mix** bears flowers in pink, red, yellow and orange with silky, wavy-edged petals. The compact plants grow 20–25 cm (8–10") tall.

Problems & Pests

California poppy generally has few pest problems, but fungi may cause trouble occasionally.

Calla Lily

Zantedeschia

Height: 40–90 cm (16–36") **Spread:** 20–60 cm (8–24") **Flower colour:** red, yellow, pink, purple, white, cream and orange, solid and bicolour; attractive foliage

THE NAME CALLA IS FROM THE GREEK WORD *KALOS*, MEANING "beautiful." In the language of herbs, the calla lily symbolizes magnificent beauty and savoir-faire. Calla lilies have a regal presence and evoke thoughts of formal occasions and wedding bouquets. Try planting them in the centre of an urn as the focus, surrounded with variegated trailing English ivy and asparagus fern. It is best not to overwhelm this beauty when trying to convey a pure statement of simplicity. When summer is over and a hard frost is looming nearer, bring the container into your home in a sunny location—ivy, ferns and all—until it's time to bring it outdoors once again.

Planting

Seeding: Indoors 2–3 months before planting outdoors; direct sow after last frost

Planting out: Once soil has warmed and risk of frost has passed

Spacing: 35–40 cm (14–16")

Growing

Calla lilies grow best in a sheltered location in **full sun**. The soil should be **fertile, humus-rich, moist** and **well drained**. To force dormant rhizomes prior to planting outdoors, plant each rhizome 10 cm (4") deep in a 15 cm (6") diameter pot. Water thoroughly and place the pot in a warm, bright location until new shoots appear. Water again only when shoots emerge, unless the potting mix dries out completely. Once the new foliage has completely unfurled, begin watering regularly until it is planted outdoors. When the risk of frost has passed, transplant the lily into either another decorative pot or into the ground for the growing season. Deadhead any faded flowers and stems.

Slowly reduce watering towards the end of the summer to encourage the foliage to die back. This will signal the rhizome to go back into dormancy prior to a fall frost. After a light frost, remove the yellow, decaying foliage and stems from the rhizome, being careful not to damage the roots. Wash the rhizome gently under tepid water to remove soil and debris. Dust the rhizome with a fungicide and let it cure for a week at room temperature, in a well-ventilated room. Once cured, store in a paper bag or on a

Z. hybrid (above)

Although they grow quite large, calla lilies can be grown as houseplants year-round, but benefit from spending summer outdoors.

wire tray in a cool, dark location at 5°–10° C (41°–50° F) until it's time to force them into leaf the following spring. Don't allow the rhizomes to touch while in storage to reduce the spread of disease, if present. If you want to split rhizomes in the spring prior to forcing, there should be at least one eye or growing point per piece. Leave split rhizomes to air-dry for a few days before transplanting. Large clumps can also be divided in late summer when lifted for winter storage.

Tips

Calla lilies are stunning additions to mixed beds and borders, and work well as large, colourful container specimens.

Recommended

Z. albomaculata (spotted calla, spotted arum lily) grows to 60 cm (24"), bearing creamy white flowers with white spotted, dark green leaves.

Z. x 'Black-Eyed Beauty' produces deep yellow flowers with a hint of green and a black throat. This hybrid grows to 35 cm (14").

This beautiful, exotic-looking plant was only available as a cut flower in the past. The introduction of new cultivars, however, has made it more readily available and worth planting.

Z. x 'Cameo' bears apricot flowers that pale to each flowers edge.

Z. x 'Dusty Pink' has light pink flowers.

Z. elliottiana (yellow calla, golden calla) forms a basal clump of white-spotted, dark green, heart-shaped leaves. It grows 60–90 cm (24–36") tall and spreads 20–30 cm (8–12"). This species bears yellow flowers in summer and is a parent plant of many popular hybrids.

Z. rehmannii (below)

Z. x 'Majestic Red' bears deep, dark burgundy red flowers with white-flecked foliage.

Z. x 'Mango' produces stunning orange-red, funnel shaped flowers.

Z. rehmannii (pink arum, pink calla) produces dark green leaves and small, pinkish red flowers. The species grows to 30 cm (12") tall.

Problems & Pests

Rot, *Botrytis* blight, rust and viral diseases can occur.

Z. albomaculata (above)

Candytuft

Iberis

Height: 15–30 cm (6–12") **Spread:** 20 cm (8") or more **Flower colour:** white, pink, purple, red

CANDYTUFT CONJURES UP IMAGES OF SWEET, GOOEY TREATS, BUT it is actually named for the Mediterranean area of Candia now known as Iräklion, on the island of Crete. It was imported to England from Greece during the Elizabethan period. It was then propagated and planted throughout parts of England, including the famous white gardens at Sissinghurst Castle. It's also quite at home here in Alberta. Plant candytuft where you can enjoy its sweet fragrance, and don't forget to cut a little bouquet for the house, because it benefits from light pruning to keep it blooming.

Planting

Seeding: Indoors in late winter; outdoors around last frost

Planting out: After last frost

Spacing: 15 cm (6")

Growing

Candytuft prefers to grow in **full sun** or **partial shade**. Partial shade is best if it gets very hot in your garden. Like many species in the mustard family, candytuft dislikes heat; blooming will often slow down or decrease in July and August. The soil should be of **poor** or **average fertility, well drained** and have a **neutral** or **alkaline pH**.

Deadheading when the seeds begin to form will keep candytuft blooming, but do let some plants go to seed to guarantee repeat performances.

Tips

This informal plant can be used on rock walls, in mixed containers or as edging for beds.

Recommended

I. umbellata (globe candytuft) has flowers in shades of pink, purple, red or white. The plant grows 15–30 cm (6–12") tall and spreads 20 cm (8") or more. **'Dwarf Fairy'** ('Dwarf Fairyland') is a compact plant that bears many flowers in a variety of pastel shades. **Flash Series** cultivars bear flowers in bright pink, purple and red.

Problems & Pests

Keep an eye open for slugs and snails. Caterpillars can also be a problem. In poorly drained soil, fungal problems may develop.

I. umbellata (photos this page)

If your candytuft seems to be blooming less often as summer progresses, trim it back lightly to promote new growth and more flowers.

Canna Lily

Canna

Height: 1–2 m (3½–6½') **Spread:** 50–90 cm (20–36") **Flower colour:** red, yellow, coral, pink, orange; attractive foliage

IT'S NOT UNCOMMON TO SEE CANNAS PLANTED IN A DRAMATIC way, adorning the entrances of restaurants and retail outlets. They are equally dramatic when grown in your own backyard.

Cannas make us think of tropical settings and the Mediterranean, and the tropical theme has become a popular trend recently. I remember the first time I noticed cannas growing in Edmonton. The canna lilies were clearly the focal point of two large, exquisite decorative pots, positioned just outside the doors of a trendy restaurant. They were meant to get your attention and it surely worked. Each pot held huge canna lilies bearing deep red flowers and large burgundy foliage, surrounded by sweet Caroline potato vine and red flowering verbena. It's something I'll never forget.

Canna species are native to Central and South America and are prized for their dramatic foliage and odd flowers, which are attractive to hummingbirds and bats.

Planting

Seeding: Indoors 1^1/$_2$–2 months before planting outdoors; direct sow after last frost

Planting out: Once soil has warmed and risk of frost has passed

Spacing: 45–60 cm (18–24")

Growing

Canna lilies grow best in **full sun**. The soil should be **fertile, moist** and **well drained**. Plant out in spring, once soil has warmed. Plants can be started early indoors in containers to get a head start on the growing season. Deadhead regularly to prolong blooming. Once all of the buds have opened and flowers are finished, remove the stalk down to the next side shoot. Division should take place in the spring. Allow the cut areas of the newly divided pieces to dry for at least 24 hours before planting.

Plant the rhizomes only deep enough to cover the top with soil. They prefer to be shallowly planted,

C. 'King Humbert' (photos this page)

approximately 10 cm (4") deep. The rhizomes should lay flat when planting, covered with no more than 5 cm (2") of good quality potting mix or soil. Transplant cannas earlier than June to ensure flowering before the end of the season.

Tips

Canna lilies can be grown in a bed or border. They make dramatic specimen plants and can even be included in large planters.

Recommended

C. '**Black Knight**' has deep bronze foliage and bears dark red flowers from mid-summer to late fall.

C. '**King Humbert**' (Roi Humbert, Red King Humbert) produces dark bronze-purple foliage and red flowers. It can reach 2 m (6') tall or more.

The **Liberty Series** offers nine cultivars in varied bicoloured combinations of red, yellow, orange, coral and pink.

C. 'King Humbert' (above), *C.* hybrids (below & right)

The foliage varies as well, including cultivars with green, burgundy and bronze leaves.

The **Pfitzer Series** of canna lilies are dwarf varieties and won't grow more than 90 cm (36") tall. **'Pfitzer's Chinese Coral'** produces grey-green foliage and coral pink flowers. **'Pfitzer's Primrose Yellow'** bears yellow blooms.

C. **'Richard Wallace'** is another tall, green-leaved hybrid with bright yellow flowers with wavy petal edges and subtle red spotting in the throat.

C. **'Stuttgart'** has dark green leaves with cream variegations and white stripes. The smaller flowers are apricot in colour. This hybrid is best grown in a location with light shade to prevent the foliage from scorching.

C. **'The President'** is a tall hybrid that grows 1.2–1.5 m (4–5') tall, bearing red flowers and blue-green leaves.

Problems & Pests

Rust, fungal leaf spot and bacterial blight.

The rhizomes can be lifted after the foliage dies back in fall. Clean off any clinging dirt and store them in a cool, frost-free location in slightly moist peat moss. Check on them regularly through the winter and if they are starting to sprout, pot them and move them to a bright window until they can be moved outdoors.

Cape Daisy
African Daisy, Monarch of the Veldt
Arctotis (Venidium)

Height: 30–60 cm (12–24") **Spread:** 30–40 cm (12–16") **Flower colour:** pink, orange, yellow, red, white; attractive foliage

THE GENUS *ARCTOTIS* IS MADE UP OF APPROXIMATELY 50 SPECIES of annuals and perennials. Most of the perennials are also commonly grown as annuals, however. This group is native to regions of South Africa with stony soils and extreme heat and environmental conditions. Cape daisies bloom for quite some time, throughout the entire summer and into fall. This exotic daisy-like flower is stunning when arranged in a bouquet with other silvery leaved plants and crisp white blossoms. True sun worshippers, cape daisies will take on the hottest locations and thrive in the sunshine, but close up their blossoms on cloudy days.

Cape daisies make interesting cut flowers, but they close up at night and in rooms that are not very bright.

Planting

Seeding: Indoors in early spring; direct sow after last frost

Planting out: Once soil has warmed

Spacing: 30–40 cm (12–16")

Growing

Choose a location in **full sun**. The soil should be **average, moist** and **well drained**. Cape daisies don't mind sandy soil, and they tolerate drought well. Keep the plants deadheaded and they will flower continuously from mid-summer to frost.

Seeds started indoors should be planted in peat pots or peat pellets to avoid disturbing the roots when transplanting. Cape daisy seeds do not keep long, so purchase or collect new seeds each year.

Tips

Cape daisies can be grouped or massed in beds, borders and cutting gardens. They do quite well when grown in planters and other containers. You can try growing a fall crop—sow seeds directly in the garden in mid-summer and enjoy the flowers throughout fall.

Recommended

A. fastuosa (monarch of the veldt, cape daisy) has bright orange flowers with a purple spot at the base of each petal. It grows 30–60 cm (12–24") tall and spreads 30 cm (12"). **'Zulu Prince'** bears large cream white or yellow flowers with bands of brown and orange at the base of each petal. The deeply lobed leaves are covered in soft hairs of silvery white.

A. fastuosa 'Zulu Prince' (above), *A.* hybrid (below)

A. x *hybrida* (Harlequin Hybrids) grow up to 50 cm (20") tall and spread 30 cm (12"). They do not come true from seed and are propagated by cuttings. The striking flowers may be pink, red, white, orange or yellow.

A. stoechadifolia var. *grandis* (blue-eyed African daisy) has 7.5 cm (3") wide, white blooms with a yellow ring, and the undersides of the petals are pale lavender blue. The plant has a nice bushy form and grows 60 cm (24") tall and 40 cm (16") wide.

Problems & Pests

Watch for aphids, leaf miners, downy mildew and leaf spot.

China Aster

Callistephus

Height: 15–90 cm (6–36") **Spread:** 25–45 cm (10–18") **Flower colour:** purple, blue, pink, red, white, peach, yellow

CHINA ASTER IS KNOWN FOR ITS GORGEOUS, MUM-LIKE BLOOMS in deep rich colours. *Callistephus* is Greek for "beautiful crown," and when you see colourful pompon- and spider-like flowers it's not difficult to understand why the Greeks felt the way they did. China asters, although lovely, do not bloom for very long so it is a good idea to plant early and late blooming selections to achieve a longer show. Prior to the 20th century, China asters were not grown as a cut flower but strictly for garden embellishment. This has changed, however, as new breeding has resulted in longer stems and bigger flowers. The flowers are now commonly used in fresh arrangements, bringing their unique attributes indoors for all to enjoy.

Planting

Seeding: Indoors in late winter; direct sow after last frost

Planting out: Once soil has warmed

Spacing: 15–30 cm (6–12")

Growing

China aster prefers **full sun** but tolerates **partial shade**. The soil should be **fertile, evenly moist, well drained** and of **neutral** or **alkaline pH**. China asters are heavy feeders, so plant them in fertile soil or fertilize regularly to get flowers like those you see in catalogues.

Start seeds in peat pots or peat pellets, because this plant doesn't like having its roots disturbed. China aster forms a shallow root system that dries out quickly during dry spells; mulch to conserve moisture.

Tips

China aster puts on a bright display when planted in groups. The plants are available in three height groups: dwarf, medium and tall. Use dwarf and medium varieties as edging plants and the taller varieties for cut-flower arrangements. Tall varieties may require staking.

Recommended

C. chinensis is the source of many varieties and cultivars. **'Comet'** is an early-flowering cultivar, growing about 25 cm (10") tall, with large, quilled double flowers in white, yellow, pink, purple, red or blue. **'Duchess'** plants are wilt resistant. The sturdy stems, up to 60 cm (24") tall, bear colourful flowers with petals that curve in towards the centre. **'Meteor'** has plants up to 90 cm (36") tall.

C. chinensis hybrids (photos this page)

The large flowers, up to 10 cm (4") across, are bright red with yellow centres. **'Pot 'n Patio'** is a popular dwarf cultivar that has double flowers and grows 15–20 cm (6–8") tall, with an equal spread. **'Princess'** grows up to 60 cm (24") tall and bears quilled, double or semi-double flowers in a wide range of colours.

Problems & Pests

Wilt diseases and aster yellows can be prevented by planting China aster in different locations each year and by planting resistant varieties. Keep China aster away from calendula, which hosts potentially harmful insects and diseases.

Cigar Flower
Cuphea

Height: 15–60 cm (6–24") **Spread:** 25–90 cm (10–36") **Flower colour:** red, pink, purple, violet, green, white

CIGAR FLOWER IS OFTEN FOUND GROWING IN CONTAINERS OF ALL sizes and shapes. Hanging baskets, in particular, take advantage of its trailing growth habit and fun flowers, which closely resemble tiny, lit cigars. This novelty plant has gained acceptance throughout the prairies over the years and is loved by children. Anything that conjures up images of Mickey Mouse is sure to be adored by the little ones and *C. llavea*, or tiny mice, is no exception. All the species listed in the Recommended section generally perform very well in warm weather and grow best in dappled sun, but not direct sun all day, which tends to make the leaf colour fade a bit.

Planting

Seeding: Sow seed indoors in early spring, approximately 8–10 weeks before the last frost date

Planting out: After risk of frost has passed

Spacing: 25–60 cm (10–24")

Growing

Cigar flower prefers **full sun to partial shade** in **moderately fertile, well-drained** soil. It does best with regular watering but can handle short periods of dryness. Batface cuphea, in particular, can really take the heat.

Tips

Cigar flowers are excellent plants for containers of all descriptions. The container can be brought into the house for the winter and kept in a sunny window. They are also effective in the annual or mixed border and as edging and perfect for hanging baskets.

Recommended

C. hybrida '**Purple Trailing**' is a vigorous grower reaching 15–30 cm (6–12") tall and 25–35 cm (10–14") wide. It has lavender blooms, dark green foliage and works well in hanging baskets and mixed containers.

C. hyssopifolia (Mexican heather, false heather, elfin herb) is a bushy, much-branched plant that forms a flat-topped mound 30–60 cm (12–24") tall and slightly wider than the height. The flowers have green calyces and light purple, pink and sometimes white petals. The plants bloom from summer to frost. '**Allyson Purple**' ('Allyson') grows 15–30 cm (6–12") tall and bears

C. llavea 'Batface' (above)
C. hybrida cultivar (below)

lavender flowers. **'Desert Snow'** has white flowers.

C. ignea (*C. platycentra*; cigar flower, firecracker plant) is a spreading, freely branching plant 30–60 cm (12–24") tall and 30–90 cm (12–36") wide. The common names relate to the thin, tubular flowers of bright red that are borne freely from late spring to frost. It can also be used as a houseplant.

C. llavea (batface cuphea, St. Peter plant, tiny mice) is a mounding to spreading plant 30–45 cm (12–18") tall and 30–60 cm (12–24") wide. It produces an abundance of flowers with green to violet calyces and bright red petals. The two longest stamens are bearded purple, making the flower look like the face of a bat or mouse. This plant can really take the heat. **'Batface'** grows 15–30 cm (6–12") tall and has a purple "face" with red "ears."

C. llavea 'Batface' (above)
C. hyssopifolia 'Allyson' (below)

C. x *purpurea* is a cross between *C. llavea* and *C. procumbens.* '**Firecracker Red Hood**' grows 25–35 cm (10–14") tall. It has tubular flowers with purple ribs and protruding red petals. '**Firefly**' has magenta red flowers. '**Summer Medley**' is a neat, mounding plant, 30–45 cm (12–18") tall, with violet and red flowers.

Problems & Pests

Problems with whiteflies, aphids, root rot, powdery mildew and leaf spot are possible.

These wonderful plants will attract hummingbirds and butterflies to your garden.

C. ignea (photos this page)

Cleome
Spider Flower
Cleome

Height: 30 cm–1.5 m (1–5') **Spread:** 45–90 cm (18–36") **Flower colour:** pink, rose, violet, white; attractive foliage

THE BEAUTY AND AIRINESS OF THIS COTTAGE-GARDEN ANNUAL has made it a staple in many a garden over the years. Its alternative common name, spider flower, is derived from its loose blossom clusters of individual flowers, which resemble the wiry legs of a spider.

The fragrant flowers are feathery and attractive to butterflies, and look wonderful mass planted in a variety of colours right beside a large grouping of tall nicotiana. Cleome is truly easy to grow and can be directly sowed into the garden. The seed requires light to germinate and consistent moisture, but little else. There's no stopping cleome once it begins to take off.

The flowers can be cut for fresh arrangements although the plants have an unusual smell that is very noticeable up close.

Planting

Seeding: Indoors in late winter; direct sow in spring

Planting out: After last frost

Spacing: 45–75 cm (18–30")

Growing

Cleomes prefer **full sun** but tolerate partial shade. Any kind of soil will do fine. Mix in plenty of organic matter to help the soil retain moisture. These plants are drought tolerant but look and perform better if watered regularly. Don't water them excessively or they will become leggy. Chill the seeds overnight prior to planting.

Pinch out the centre of a cleome plant when transplanting, and it will branch out to produce up to a dozen blooms. Deadhead to prolong the blooming period.

Tips

Cleome can be planted in groups at the back of a border. These plants are also effective in the centre of an island bed; use lower-growing plants around the edges to hide the leafless lower stems of cleome.

Be careful when handling these plants because they have nasty barbs along the stems.

Recommended

C. hassleriana is a tall, upright plant with strong, supple, thorny stems. It grows up to 1.5 m (5') tall. The foliage and flowers of this plant have a strong, but not unpleasant, scent. **'Helen Campbell'** has white flowers. **Royal Queen Series** has

C. hassleriana (photos this page)

flowers in all colours, available by individual colour or a mix of colours. The varieties are named by their colour; e.g., 'Cherry Queen,' 'Rose Queen' and 'Violet Queen.' Plants in this series resist fading. **'Sparkler Blush'** is a dwarf cultivar that grows up to 90 cm (36") tall. It bears pink flowers that fade to white.

C. serrulata (Rocky Mountain bee plant) is native to western North America. It is rarely available commercially, but the dwarf cultivar **'Solo'** is available to be grown from seed. It grows 30–45 cm (12–18") tall and bears 5–7 cm (2–3") pink and white blooms. This plant is thornless.

C. *hassleriana* 'Helen Campbell' (above)
C. *hassleriana* (below)

Problems & Pests

Aphids may be a problem.

"Hummingbird flower" might be a more appropriate name for these plants. They bloom through the fall, providing nectar for the tiny birds after many other flowers have finished blooming.

C. hassleriana Royal Queen Series (above)
C. hassleriana (below)

Clover

Trifolium

Height: 8–30 cm (3–10") **Spread:** 30–45 cm (10–18") **Flower colour:** white, inconspicuous; grown for its foliage

WE'VE ALL LIKELY EXPERIENCED THE FRAGRANCE OF CLOVER WHEN driving along the road out in the country, but have you ever thought that clover might also be a great little plant for your containers? Granted the type recommended here is much more ornate than the species considered weeds by most gardeners. This clover is colourful and ideal for containers of any size or shape. Walking through a field of clover, you'll see hundreds of honey bees, because clover blossoms are one of their favourites. Pendent florets have been emptied of their nectar, while the ones still full of nectar stand tall. *Trifolium repens* may not flower in our short season, but even without flowers, this member of the newly trendy black plants group is sure to please.

Planting

Seeding: Not recommended

Planting out: Once the risk of frost has passed

Spacing: 20–25 cm (8–10")

Growing

Black-leaved clover is best grown in **full to partial sun**. The soil should be **moist** but **well drained** and with a **neutral pH**.

Tips

This lovely little plant will add interest to containers or the edge of mixed borders. It's especially striking when planted next to other dramatically coloured foliage and bright, contrasting flowers. It also works well in trough and rock gardens. Because of its invasive nature, clover is often best grown in containers and areas where it won't be able to stray.

Recommended

T. repens is a perennial that is often grown as an annual and is rarely cultivated as a species for ornamental purposes, but the cultivars are becoming incredibly popular. Its small pompom-like flowers can be pink, red, yellow and white. **'Aureum'** produces large gold-veined leaflets. **'Dark Dancer'** (Atropurpureum), has a dwarf habit and deep, dark burgundy leaves edged in lime green. **'Purpurescens Quadrifolium'** is a fast-growing tender perennial that produces typical clover leaves with dark burgundy centres surrounded by bright green. It may produce small, pea-like white flowers in late summer, but they are rather small.

T. repens 'Purpurescens Quadrifolium' (photos this page)

Problems and Pests

Powdery mildew, rust and fungal problems are all possibilities, but remote.

The Trifolium *genus encompasses all clovers.* Trifolium *plants have spreading growth habits, and each stem can produce three to five leaflets. Retailers often refer to* Trifolium *specimens as "clover-like" or lump them into the* Oxalis *group so as not to scare away gardeners who fear clover.*

Cobbitty Daisy

Marguerite Daisy

Argyranthemum

Height: 30–60 cm (12–24") **Spread:** 30–60 cm (12–24") **Flower colour:** white, pink, yellow, apricot, purple; attractive foliage

COBBITTY DAISIES PRODUCE SIMPLY THE MOST OUTSTANDING summer blooms when the nights remain cool, as they often are in Alberta. *Argyranthemum* includes over 20 species originating in the Canary Islands and Madeira, an island in the Atlantic off the coast of Morocco, where average summer temperatures are similar to those in Alberta. *Argyranthemum* species were once part of the genus *Chrysanthemum*, and are also commonly known as Marguerite daisy. These plants are incredibly easy to grow but are heavy feeders, and will require regular fertilizing to maintain their prolific blooming cycle. The flowers can be used in fresh arrangements, but they shouldn't be mixed with other cut flowers because they will cause them to wilt.

Planting

Seeding: Sow indoors 1–2 months before last frost, or directly once the soil has warmed

Planting out: Once the soil has warmed

Spacing: 30–45 cm (12–18")

Growing

Cobbitty daisies prefer **full sun** but tolerate **partial shade**. The soil should be **moderately fertile** and **well drained**.

Tips

Cobbitty daisies are ideal for containers, including window boxes. They are also quite effective in mixed beds and borders in small groupings or en masse. Some of the cultivars grow lower to the ground with a spreading habit, making them suitable edging annuals. Cobbitty daisies are tolerant to extreme heat and will bloom prolifically without deadheading but can appear untidy when spent flowers are left on the plant.

Recommended

A. frutescens is a subshrub grown as an annual but is rarely available in cultivation. It produces ornate, deeply divided leaves and single daisy-like flowers in white with bright yellow centres. Hybrids and cultivars are abundant in their selection and very popular. **'Butterfly'** bears canary yellow flowers and grows 30–45 cm (12–18") tall. The **'Comet'** series offers two selections in a single white variation and a single pink. **'Creme'** produces large pale yellow, single flowers. **'Gypsy Rose'** bears deep, dark pink blooms with bright

A. frutescens 'Butterfly'

yellow centres that fade to a medium pink. **'Midas Gold'** bears butter yellow petals that fade to cream, surrounding a bronze centre. This cultivar grows 45–60 cm (18–24") tall. **'Sugar Baby'** has white petals surrounding a yellow centre in a single form while **'Summer Melody'** produces tightly packed, double, pink flowers. **'Think Pink'** has pale pink, mounded flowers; **'Vanilla Butterfly'** is a white version of 'Butterfly,' and which bears large, rich cream-coloured flowers.

A. x **'Mary Wootton'** bears light pink flowers that fade almost to white over time with pink disk florets in the centre. This hybrid can grow up to 90 cm (36") in the right conditions.

Problems & Pests

Crown gall and chrysanthemum leaf miners are possibilities, but are rare to infrequent.

Coleus

Solenostemon (Coleus)

Height: 15–90 cm (6–36") or more **Spread:** usually equal to height
Flower colour: light purple; plant grown for foliage

ONCE UPON A TIME, THERE WERE ONLY A FEW COLEUS SELECTIONS
to choose from, but that has all changed, and for the better. Plant breeders
have been busily creating new, colourful, one-of-a-kind combinations, with
velvety leaf shapes and forms both eccentric and peculiar. Retro isn't back
only in interior design and fashion, but in plants as well. Coleus is truly one
of the plants of the new gardening millennia, as trends are going in the
direction of deep, dark colour saturation and strange new combinations
never thought possible, especially in an annual. Coleus is easily paired with
just about anything, but looks fantastic when planted in large containers
with foliage and flowers of a similar colour, such as 'Amber Waves' and
'Amethyst Myst' *Heuchera* (coral bells), 'Toffee Twist' *Carex* (sedge),
'Sundaze Bronze' *Bracteantha* (strawflower) and 'Sedona' *Coleus*.

Planting

Seeding: Indoors in winter

Planting out: Once soil has warmed

Spacing: 30 cm (12")

Growing

Seed-grown coleus prefers to grow in **light** or **partial shade** but tolerates full shade if the shade isn't too dense, and full sun if the plants are watered regularly. Cultivars propagated from cuttings thrive in full sun to partial shade. The soil for all coleus should be of **rich to average fertility, humus rich, moist** and **well drained.**

S. scutellarioides cultivars (photos this page)

Although coleus is a member of the mint family, with the characteristic square stems, it has none of the enjoyable culinary or aromatic qualities.

Place the seeds in a refrigerator for one or two days before planting them on the soil surface; the cold temperatures will assist in breaking the seeds' dormancy. They need light to germinate. Seedlings will be green at first, but leaf variegation will develop as the plants mature.

Coleus is easy to propagate from stem cuttings, and by doing so you can ensure that you have a group of plants with the same leaf markings, shapes or colours. As your seedlings develop, decide which you like best, and when they are about three pairs of leaves high, pinch off the tip. The plants will begin to branch out.

Pinch all the tips off regularly as the branches grow. This process will produce a very bushy plant from which you will be able to take a large number of cuttings. The cuttings should be about three leaf pairs long. Make the cut just below a leaf pair, and then remove the two bottom leaves. Plant the cuttings in pots filled with a soil mix intended for starting seeds. Keep the soil moist

S. scutellarioides cultivar (photos this page)

but not soggy. The plants should develop roots within a couple of weeks.

Tips

The bold, colourful foliage makes coleus dramatic when the plants are grouped together as edging plants or in beds, borders or mixed containers. Coleus can also be grown indoors as a houseplant in a bright room.

When flower buds develop, it is best to pinch them off, because the plants tend to stretch out and become less attractive after they flower.

Recommended

S. scutellarioides (*Coleus blumei* var. *verschaffeltii*) forms a bushy mound of foliage. The leaf edges range from slightly toothed to very ruffled. The leaves are usually multi-coloured with shades ranging from pale greenish yellow to deep purple-black. The size may be 15–90 cm (6–36"), depending on the cultivar, and the spread is usually equal to the height. Dozens of cultivars are available, but many cannot be started from seed. The following cultivars can be started from seed: the **Dragon Series**, with bright yellow-green margins around variably coloured leaves; '**Garnet Robe,**' with a cascading habit and dark wine red leaves edged with yellow-green; '**Molten Lava,**' with dark red leaves; '**Palisandra,**' with velvety, purple-black foliage; '**Scarlet Poncho,**' with wine red leaves edged with yellow-green; and the **Wizard Series**, with variegated foliage on compact plants.

Problems & Pests

Mealybugs, scale insects, aphids and whiteflies can cause occasional trouble.

Coleus can be trained to grow into a standard (tree) form. Pinch off the lower leaves and side branches as they grow to create a long bare stem with leaves only on the upper half. Once the plant reaches the desired height, pinch from the top to create a bushy rounded crown.

S. scutellarioides cultivar (above), Wizard Series (below)

Corn Cockle

Agrostemma

Height: 60–90 cm (24–36") **Spread:** 30 cm (12") **Flower colour:** purple, pink, white

SOME PRAIRIE GARDENERS SEE THIS FIVE-PETALLED BEAUTY AS a weed. However, it's considered a field weed only in parts of Europe and is fully appreciated as a charming annual in Alberta. It's not often found in garden centres as a bedding plant, but its seed is readily available. Corn cockle is easily sown directly into the ground and will quickly begin to perform. If there ever was a plant that screamed out "cottage garden," this would surely be the one. The jewel-toned flowers against the silvery foliage are not only beautiful when planted en masse in the garden, but are equally as delightful when cut and added to fresh floral arrangements. The flowers will not only attract the attention of passersby, but also bees and most pollinating insects, creating a flurry of activity within your very own prairie cottage garden.

Planting

Seeding: Direct sow around last frost date or start indoors about a month earlier

Planting out: After last frost

Spacing: 20–30 cm (8–12")

Growing

Corn cockle grows best in **full sun**. The soil should be of **poor fertility** and **well drained**. This plant prefers cool weather and may stop flowering during the hottest part of summer. Insert twiggy stakes around young plants to provide support as they grow. Deadhead to prolong blooming and prevent self-seeding.

Tips

Corn cockle makes a good companion plant for bushy, silver-leaved perennials such as artemisias. The bright flowers stand out against the grey, and the stiffer perennial will support the weaker-stemmed annual. Corn cockle also makes a good filler plant for the middle of the border.

If you have a cutting garden, add corn cockle to the mix. Fresh cuts harvested just as the flowers open will last five days or more in a floral arrangement.

The seeds can cause stomachaches if ingested.

Recommended

A. githago is an upright plant with grey-green leaves and purple or white flowers. **'Milas'** ('Rose Queen') bears dark purple-pink flowers. **'Ocean Pearls'** ('Pearl') grows to 90 cm (36") tall, producing silky white flowers with black flecks. **'Purple**

A. githago (above), A. githago 'Milas' (below)

Foam' produces lavender blooms and silver foliage. It grows 60–90 cm (24–36") tall.

Problems & Pests

Rare problems with leaf spot are possible.

Corn cockle flowers attract butterflies to the garden. The nectar tube of the flower may be a little too deep for bees.

Cosmos

Cosmos

Height: 30 cm–2 m (1–6½') **Spread:** 30–45 cm (12–18") **Flower colour:**
white, yellow, gold, orange, shades of pink and of red; attractive foliage

COSMOS HAS BEEN CULTIVATED FOR GENERATIONS AND HAS AN
interesting history. Spanish priests grew cosmos in their mission gardens in
Mexico. The evenly placed petals led them to christen the flower *cosmos*,
from the Greek meaning harmony. Little did I know that I would still have
cosmos growing along my driveway after carefully sowing the seed over
10 years ago. They are wonderful self-seeders and produce beautiful, light,
airy stems with brilliant daisy-like flowers. Cosmos reach their peak in the
warm days of fall, when they become one of the majestic flowers in the
landscape. When cosmos are given plenty of room, they branch freely, producing abundant flowers. And for those chocolate lovers out there, don't
overlook *C. atrosanguineus*, as it has the most delicious aroma, reminiscent
of sweet, creamy chocolate.

Planting

Seeding: Indoors in late winter; direct sow after soil has warmed

Planting out: After last frost

Spacing: 30–45 cm (12–18")

Growing

Cosmos like **full sun**. The soil should be of **poor** or **average fertility** and **well drained**. Cosmos are drought tolerant. Overfertilizing and over-watering can reduce the number of flowers produced. Yellow cosmos (*C. sulphureus*) will do better if sown directly in the garden. Keep faded blooms cut to encourage more buds. Often, these plants reseed themselves.

Cosmos plants are likely to need staking but are difficult to stake. If you want to avoid staking, plant cosmos

C. bipinnatus (photos this page)

Cosmos flowers make lovely, long-lasting fillers in flower arrangements.

C. atrosanguineus (above), C. bipinnatus (below)

in a sheltered location or against a fence. You could also grow shorter varieties. If staking can't be avoided, push twiggy branches into the ground when the plants are young and allow them to grow up between the branches. The branches will be hidden by the mature plants.

Tips

Cosmos is attractive in cottage gardens, at the back of a border or mass planted in an informal bed or border.

Recommended

C. atrosanguineus (chocolate cosmos) has recently become popular among annual connoisseurs for its fragrant, deep maroon flowers that some claim smells like chocolate. The plant is upright, growing to 75 cm (30") tall, but tends to flop over a bit when the stem gets too long.

C. bipinnatus (annual cosmos) has many cultivars. The flowers come in magenta, rose, pink or white, usually with yellow centres. Old varieties grow 90 cm–1.8 m (3–6') tall, while some of the newer cultivars grow 30–90 cm (12–36") tall. **'Daydream'** has white flowers flushed with pink at the petal bases. It grows up to 1.5 m (5') tall. **'Psyche'** bears large, showy, semi-double flowers in pink, white and red. **Sea Shells Series** has flowers in all colours and petals that are rolled into tubes. It grows up to about 1 m (42") tall. **Sensation Mix** bears large, white or pink flowers and grows up to 1.2 m (4') tall. **Sonata Series** has red, pink or white flowers on compact plants up to 60 cm (24") tall.

C. sulphureus (yellow cosmos) has gold, orange, scarlet and yellow flowers. Old varieties grow 2 m (6½') tall, and new varieties grow 30 cm–1.2 m (1–4') tall. **'Klondike'** is a compact cultivar about 30–60 cm (12–24") tall. Its single or semi-double flowers are bright yellow or orange-red. **Ladybird Series** has compact dwarf plants, 30–60 cm (12–24") tall, that rarely need staking. The foliage is not as feathery as it is in other cultivars.

Problems & Pests

Cosmos rarely have any problems, but watch for wilt, aster yellows, powdery mildew and aphids.

C. sulphureus (above), *C. bipinnatus* (below)

Cup-and-Saucer Vine
Cathedral Bells
Cobaea

Height: 1.8–7.5 m (6–25') or more **Spread:** equal to height, if trained
Flower colour: green, maturing to purple or white

THIS NATIVE OF MEXICO WAS A GARDEN FAVOURITE DURING THE
Victorian era because of its prolific blooming habit and classic appearance.
It is equally as popular today for the same reasons and is a staple on the
prairie landscape. Cup-and-saucer vine needs little else to get going other
than a stable support. It is important, however, to start this annual from
seed indoors prior to the last frost of spring, or to begin with young
seedlings. Doing so ensures that they flower long before the first fall frost
hits. Decorative seedpods form once the flower has
fallen away, providing additional
interest into fall.

Planting

Seeding: Indoors in mid-winter

Planting out: After last frost

Spacing: 30 cm (12")

Growing

Cup-and-saucer vine prefers **full sun**. It is fond of hot weather and will do best if planted in a sheltered site with southern exposure. The soil should be **moist, well drained** and of **average fertility**. Keep the vine well watered and avoid overfertilizing. Too much nitrogen causes it to grow vigorously but also delays flowering. Set the seeds on edge when planting them, and barely cover them with soil.

Tips

Cup-and-saucer vine requires a sturdy support in order to climb, so grow it up a trellis, over an arbor or along a chain-link fence. It uses grabbing hooks to climb, so it won't be able to grow up a wall without something to grab.

Recommended

C. scandens is a vigorous climbing vine from Mexico. Its flowers are creamy green when they open and mature to deep purple. **Var.** *alba* has white flowers. A new variety called **'Key Lime'** produces elegant pale green, bell-shaped flowers on long, twining stems. **'Royal Plum'** blossoms mature from green to a rich purple.

Problems & Pests

This plant may have trouble with aphids.

C. scandens (photos this page)

The genus name, Cobaea, *is derived from the name of the 18th-century Spanish Jesuit missionary and botanist, Father Bernado Coba.* Scandens *is from the Latin for "climbing."*

Cup Flower

Nierembergia

Height: 15–30 cm (6–12") **Spread:** 15–30 cm (6–12") **Flower colour:** blue, purple or white, with yellow centres

CUP FLOWER IS IDEAL FOR PLANTING AROUND THE BARE SPOTS surrounding perennials that are looking spent or have finished their blooming cycle, including irises, daylilies and peonies. The flowers and leaves contrast nicely with the bolder foliage and offer something more than just green leaves with cut off stems. The cup flowers can be pulled out in the fall and your perennials will then be ready to be cut back in preparation for the fall and winter months.

Planting

Seeding: Indoors in mid-winter

Planting out: Spring

Spacing: 15–30 cm (6–12")

Growing

Cup flower grows well in **full sun** or **partial shade**. The soil should be of **average fertility, moist** and **well drained**. Fertilize little, if at all.

Tips

Use cup flower as an annual ground-cover. It is also useful for the edges of beds and borders, in rock gardens, on rock walls and in containers and hanging baskets. It grows best when summers are cool, and it can withstand a light frost.

Recommended

N. **'Blue Eyes'** is a new, larger-growing variety with lacy leaves and large, white flowers with a blue, star-shaped eye. It loves heat and humidity and works well as a mid-range plant in a container or as a mid-border plant.

N. caerulea (*N. hippomanica*) forms a small mound of foliage. This plant bears delicate, cup-shaped flowers in lavender blue with yellow centres. **'Mont Blanc'** is an All-America Selections winner bearing white flowers with yellow centres.

N. frutescens **'Purple Robe'** is a dense, compact plant producing deep purple flowers with golden eyes.

Problems & Pests

Slugs are likely to be the worst problem for this plant. Because cup flower is susceptible to tobacco mosaic virus, don't plant it near any flowering tobacco or tomato plants.

N. caerulea 'Mont Blanc' (photos this page)

Cup flowers belong to the highly poisonous nightshade family, so be sure to keep them away from children and pets.

Dahlberg Daisy
Golden Fleece
Thymophylla

Height: 15–30 cm (6–12") **Spread:** 30 cm (12") **Flower colour:** yellow, less commonly orange; attractive foliage

THIS MEMBER OF THE *ASTERACEAE* FAMILY IS A TOUGH LITTLE annual. Its native home and habitat should be some indication. There aren't many plants that can tolerate the dry slopes and prairies in Texas, Mexico and Central America. This vigorous little plant is a prolific bloomer and the perfect filler plant in containers and mixed beds. It grows to a medium size and fills in the gaps between taller plants and creepers, displaying a profusion of bright yellow, daisy-like blossoms atop ferny foliage that's aromatic and tough as nails.

T. tenuiloba

Planting

Seeding: Indoors in mid-winter; direct sow in spring

Planting out: After last frost

Spacing: 20–30 cm (8–12")

Growing

Plant Dahlberg daisy in **full sun**. Any **well-drained** soil is suitable, although soil of **poor** or **average fertility** is preferred. Dahlberg daisy prefers cool summers. In hot climates, it flowers in spring or late summer and fall.

Direct-sown plants may not flower until quite late in summer. For earlier blooms, start the seeds indoors. Don't cover the seeds, because they require light to germinate. Dahlberg daisies may self-sow and reappear each year. Trimming your plants back when flowering seems to be slowing will encourage new growth and more blooms.

Tips

This attractive plant can be used along the edges of borders, along the tops of rock walls, or in hanging baskets or mixed containers. In any location where it can cascade over and trail down an edge, Dahlberg daisy will look wonderful.

Recommended

T. tenuiloba (*Dyssodia tenuiloba*) forms a mound of ferny foliage. It produces many bright yellow, daisy-like flowers from spring until the summer heat causes it to fade. Trim it back once the flowers fade, and it may revive in late summer as the weather cools.

Dahlberg daisy has fragrant foliage that some people compare to a lemon thyme scent. Perhaps this is the origin of the name Thymophylla, *"thyme-leaf."*

Dianthus
Sweet William
Dianthus

Height: 15–30 cm (6–30") **Spread:** 20–30 cm (8–12") **Flower colour:** white, pink, red, purple

THE GENUS *DIANTHUS* INCLUDES PLANTS SUCH AS CARNATIONS and pinks. This group of perennials, biennials and annuals has been a garden favourite for generations. They're easy to identify by their sweet clove-like scent, and bees and butterflies love to gather to feed on their flowerheads. Dianthus plants have a reputation for self-seeding but are not considered to be invasive, spreading only moderately. With such an array of species, hybrids and cultivars to choose from, it's hard to imagine a prairie garden without a touch of dianthus.

Planting

Seeding: Sow seed in late spring to early summer for bloom the following year; sow seed of *D. chinensis* in fall or indoors in spring

Transplanting: Spring

Spacing: 15–30 cm (6–12")

Growing

Dianthus prefers **full sun** but tolerates some light shade. A **light, neutral** or **alkaline, humus-rich, well-drained** soil is preferred. The most important factor in the successful cultivation of dianthus is drainage. Mix gravel into its area of the flowerbed to encourage good drainage. Growing these plants in slightly alkaline soil will produce excellent colour over a long period.

Deadhead as the flowers fade to prolong blooming. Leave a few flowers in place to go to seed, and the plants will self-seed quite easily. Seedlings may differ from the parent plants, often with new and interesting results.

D. 'Telstar Pink' (above), *D. chinensis* cultivars (below)

The tiny, delicate petals of pinks can be used to decorate cakes. Be sure to remove the bitter white part at the base of the petals before using them.

Tips

Dianthus are great for mass planting, edging flower borders and walkways. Use dianthus in the rock garden or try these plants for cut flowers.

Keep sheltered from strong winds and the hottest afternoon sun.

Recommended

D. barbatus (sweet William) is a biennial mostly grown as an annual. It reaches a height of 45–60 cm (18–24") tall and spreads 20–30 cm (8–12"). Flattened clusters of often two-toned white, pink, red or purple-red flowers bloom in late spring to early summer. **'Hollandia Mix'** grows to 75 cm (30") tall. **'Indian Summer'** is a compact plant, growing 15–20 cm (6–8") tall. **Roundabout Series** grows 20–30 cm (8–12") tall and produces solid or two-toned blooms in the first year

D. barbatus cultivars (photos this page)

from seed. **'Summer Beauty'**
reaches a height of 30 cm (12").

D. chinensis (China pink, annual
pink) is an erect, mound-forming
plant growing 15–75 cm (6–30") tall
and 20–30 cm (8–12") wide. The
fragrant flowers come in pink, red,
white and light purple and are produced for an extended period in late
spring and summer. There are many
cultivars available. **'Strawberry
Parfait'** is a bicoloured dianthus
with dark pink centres and pale
pink frilled edges. It grows to 20 cm
(8") tall. The **Telstar Series** are hybrids
of *D. chinensis* and *D. barbatus*,
growing 20–30 cm (8–12") tall and
wide, producing blooms in solid
and two-toned shades of pink, red
and white. They are usually listed
under *D. chinensis*.

D. 'Telstar Crimson' (above)
D. 'Corona Cherry Magic' (below)

D. 'Corona Cherry Magic' grows
20–25 cm (8–10") tall and wide and
has 6–7.5 cm (2½–3") wide flowers
that may be solid cherry red or
lavender, or bicoloured. It's a 2003
All-America Selections winner.

D. 'Rainbow Loveliness' grows to
60 cm (24") tall and bears very
fragrant flowers in shades of white,
pink and lavender.

Problems & Pests

Rust and *fusarium* wilt may be problems. Providing good drainage and
air circulation will keep most fungal
problems away. Occasional problems
with slugs, snails and sow bugs are
possible.

Dwarf Morning Glory
Bush Morning Glory
Convolvulus

Height: 15–40 cm (6–16") **Spread:** 25–30 cm (10–12") **Flower colour:** blue, purple, pink, white

DWARF MORNING GLORY IS A VERY TRADITIONAL, OLD-FASHIONED annual that has been with us for generations. From time to time it has fallen out of favour, only to be replaced with a vine that produces flowers almost identical to those of this species. This widely available and versatile annual is incredibly easy to grow, produces copious amounts of colourful flowers all summer and thrives in our sometimes harsh climate. Two easy ways to tell a common morning glory (*Ipomoea purpurea*) or morning glory (*I. tricolor*) from a dwarf morning glory (*Convolvulus tricolor*) are by height and flowering habit. *I. purpurea* and *I. tricolor* are climbers that can reach 25–75 cm (10–30') heights whereas *C. tricolor* grows only 30–40 cm (12–16") tall and doesn't climb. *I. purpurea* and *I. tricolor* flowers often open only in the morning and close by mid-afternoon while *C. tricolor* flowers stay open all day.

Planting

Seeding: Indoors in late winter; direct sow in mid- or late spring

Planting out: Mid- or late spring

Spacing: 20–30 cm (8–12")

Growing

Dwarf morning glory prefers **full sun**. The soil should be of **poor** or **average fertility** and **well drained**. This plant may not flower well in rich, moist soil.

Soak the seeds in water overnight before planting them. If starting seeds early indoors, plant them in peat pots to avoid root damage when transplanting.

Tips

Dwarf morning glory is a compact, mounding plant that can be grown on rock walls or in borders, containers or hanging baskets.

Recommended

C. tricolor bears flowers that last only a single day, blooming in the

C. tricolor 'White Ensign' (above), *C. tricolor* (below)

morning and twisting shut that evening. The species grows 30–40 cm (12–16") tall. **Ensign Series** has low-growing, spreading plants growing 15 cm (6") tall. 'Royal Ensign' has deep blue flowers with white and yellow throats. **'Star of Yalta'** bears deep purple flowers that pale to violet in the throat.

Problems & Pests

This easy-care plant is rarely plagued by pests or diseases.

Fan Flower

Scaevola

Height: up to 20 cm (8") **Spread:** up to 90 cm (36") or more
Flower colour: blue, purple; attractive foliage

THIS IS A RELATIVELY NEW ADDITION TO THE ANNUALS TABLES IN
your local garden centre, but it's a winner and here to stay. This annual is
commonly known as fan flower because all the petals are balanced on one
side, resembling little Japanese fans. Versatile and endlessly useful, this plant
is often found in hanging baskets and containers because of its trailing
habit, but it also makes an effective groundcover and works beautifully
tucked into crevices in stone walls, spilling over the rocks and displaying its
colourful fans, which wave in the slightest breeze.

*Regular pinching and
trimming will keep
your fan flower bushy
and blooming.*

Planting

Seeding: Indoors in late winter

Planting out: After last frost

Spacing: 60 cm–1.2 m (2–4')

Growing

Fan flower grows well in **full sun** or **light shade**. The soil should be of **average fertility, moist** and **well drained**. Water regularly, because this plant doesn't like to dry out completely. It does, however, recover quickly from wilting when watered.

S. aemula (photos this page)

This attractive plant is actually a perennial that is treated as an annual. Cuttings can be taken during summer and new plants grown indoors to be used the following summer, or a plant can be brought in and kept in a bright room over winter. Seeds can be difficult to find.

Tips

This plant makes an interesting addition to mixed borders, or it can be used under shrubs, where its long, trailing stems will form an attractive groundcover.

Recommended

S. aemula forms a mound of foliage from which trailing stems emerge. The fan-shaped flowers come in shades of purple, usually with white bases. The species is rarely grown because there are many improved cultivars. **'Blue Wonder,'** a Proven Winners cultivar, has long, trailing branches, making it ideal for hanging baskets. It can eventually spread 90 cm (36") or more. **'Saphira'** is a new compact variety with deep blue flowers. It spreads about 30 cm (12").

Problems & Pests

Whiteflies may cause problems for fan flower if the plant becomes stressed from lack of water.

Fan flower is native to Australia and Polynesia.

Feverfew

Tanacetum

Height: 20 cm–1.2 m (8"–4') **Spread:** 25–90 cm (10–36")
Flower colour: yellow-centred, white, pink, purple, yellow, red; attractive foliage

VALUABLE AS AN ORNAMENTAL PLANT IN ALBERTA GARDENS TODAY, feverfew has been a part of gardening in one form or another for centuries. It appeared in the seminal late 16th century botanical work, *The Herbal*, by John Gerard, one of the greatest English herbalists of his day. Mr. Gerard described feverfew's attributes in great detail, lauding it as a treatment for a variety of ailments. We've since learnt that it has few if any medicinal qualities but have discovered that pyrethrum, a derivative of the plant, effectively controls most insect pests in the garden. It is frequently used as an active ingredient in organic or natural insecticides today.

Planting

Seeding: Start seed in early spring. Soil temperature should be 10°–13° C (50°–55° F)

Planting out: Spring.

Spacing: 30–90 cm (12–36") apart

Growing

Feverfew grow best in **full sun**. Any **well-drained** soil is suitable. Very fertile soil may encourage invasive growth. Deadheading will prolong the blooming period. Divide in spring as needed to control spread and maintain plant vigour.

Tips

Use feverfew in borders, rock gardens, wildflower gardens, cottage gardens and meadow gardens.

Recommended

T. parthenium (feverfew) is a perennial that is often grown as an annual. It is a bushy plant with fern-like foliage. It grows 30–90 cm (12–36") tall, spreads 30–60 cm (12–24") and bears clusters of small, daisy-like flowers. **'Aureum'** has bright golden yellow-green foliage and single, white flowers with a hint of pale yellow. **'Ball's Double White'** has double, white flowers while **'Butterball'** bears double yellow flowers. **'Golden Ball'** forms a compact plant bearing yellow double flowers; **'Golden Moss'** is a dwarf cultivar with golden, moss-like foliage. It has a height and spread of 15 cm (6"). **'Snowball'** bears double white flowers with light yellow centres.

Problems & Pests

Feverfew is generally pest free, but keep an eye open for aphids.

T. parthenium (above)
T. parthenium 'Golden Ball' (below)

Feverfew has been used medicinally for thousands of years and grows, cultivated and wild, all over Europe and North and South America.

Flowering Flax

Linum

Height: 45–60 cm (18–24") **Spread:** 15 cm (6") **Flower colour:** pink, white, red, blue, purple

FLOWERING FLAX IS A PROLIFIC BLOOMER, WHICH MAKES UP FOR the fact that each flower lasts for only one day. There are always more to follow, however, and little can stop them but a hard fall frost. Often people confuse annual flowering flax, *L. grandiflorum*, with perennial flax, *L. perenne*. There are distinct similarities and differences, but the hardiness separates one from the other. The species grown throughout the prairies as an annual looks somewhat different than its perennial cousin, but it's just as intriguing, easy to grow and useful. The cultivars are far more common in cultivation than the species, producing scarlet red, white with brown centres and violet flowers on wispy stems.

Planting

Seeding: Direct sow in mid-spring

Planting out: Around last frost

Spacing: 10–15 cm (4–6")

Growing

Flowering flax grows well in **full sun**, but during the heat of summer it enjoys protection from the hot afternoon sun. The soil should be of **average fertility, light, humus rich** and **well drained**.

Tips

Flowering flax can be used in borders and mixed containers and will nicely fill in the spaces between young perennials and shrubs in the landscape.

Recommended

L. grandiflorum is an upright, branching plant. It grows 45–60 cm (18–24") tall and spreads about 15-cm (6"). It bears dark-centred, light pink flowers. **'Bright Eyes'** bears white flowers with dark red or brown centres. It grows about 45 cm (18") tall. **'Caeruleum'** bears blue or purple flowers. **'Rubrum'** bears deep red flowers on plants that grow 45 cm (18") tall.

Problems & Pests

Excess moisture can cause trouble with stem rot and damping off. Slugs, snails and aphids can also cause problems.

With its delicate appearance, flowering flax is a beautiful complement to plants with large, dramatic blooms.

L. grandiflorum 'Rubrum' (photos this page)

The related L. usitatissimum *is the source of the flax seeds used to produce oil and linen fibre. It has been in cultivation for more than 7000 years.*

Flowering Maple
Chinese Lantern
Abutilon

Height: 45–90 cm (18–36") **Spread:** 45–60 cm (18–24") **Flower colour:** red, pink, white, orange, yellow

WHENEVER I SEE A FLOWERING MAPLE, I THINK OF MY MOTHER and the plant that she has grown and cared for over many years. It spends the summers outdoors in the sunshine happily blooming just as it did all winter long in her home. This unique plant has been gaining popularity in the garden, although it has been sold over the years only as a houseplant. Once it made its way outside onto patios and balconies, it became a stunning addition to gardens throughout the province. It's a delight to grow and requires very little care, but gives and gives. Each variety produces an abundance of hibiscus or hollyhock-like flowers in a wide array of pink and orange shades, whether indoors or out.

This plant is in the mallow family and is not related to maples, as one of its common names suggests.

Planting

Seeding: Indoors in early winter with soil at 21°–23° C (70°–75° F); blooms in 5–6 months from seed

Planting out: After last frost

Spacing: 60 cm (24")

Growing

Flowering maple grows well in **full sun** but can benefit from some shade during the afternoon. The soil should be **average to fertile**, **moist** and **well drained**. Pinch back growing tips to encourage bushy growth.

A. x hybridum (photos this page)

Tips

Include flowering maple in borders and mixed containers. Container-grown plants are easier to bring indoors, where they will continue to bloom for most of the fall and winter. Indoor plants will need a bright window and should be allowed to dry out between waterings in winter.

Recommended

A.* x *hybridum (*A. globosum*) is a bushy, mound-forming shrub that can be treated as an annual or wintered indoors and moved outside for the summer. Drooping, cup- or trumpet-shaped flowers are borne for most of the summer. Named varieties are available, but most seed catalogues sell seeds in mixed packets, so flower colours will be a surprise.

Problems & Pests

Few problems occur in the garden, but whiteflies, mealybugs and scale insects can cause trouble when plants are moved indoors.

Forget-Me-Not
Myosotis

Height: 15–30 cm (6–12") **Spread:** 15 cm (6") or wider **Flower colour:** blue, pink, white

EACH YEAR, WHEN I RETURN HOME AT THE END OF MAY FROM the Chelsea Flower Show in England, my garden is a sea of blue, and sometimes pink. It is all because of this little plant. Forget-me-nots in bloom are always a sure sign that spring is upon us, and they fit in well with spring bulbs in shades of orange, yellow and purple. Forget-me-nots are with you forever once seeded because each plant will self-seed year after year. For this to happen, leave spent flowers on the plants well after they've faded. Doing so will also give you intermittent blooming throughout the summer.

Planting

Seeding: Direct sow in spring; indoors in early spring

Planting out: Around last frost

Spacing: 25 cm (10") apart

Growing

Forget-me-not prefers **light** or **partial shade**, but it will tolerate full sun if the soil stays moist and the weather isn't too hot. The soil should be **fertile, moist** and **well drained**. Adding lots of organic matter to the soil will help it retain moisture while maintaining good drainage.

Seeds sown in spring will flower in mid-summer or fall. Forget-me-not is a short-lived perennial that is treated as an annual. It may self-seed if faded plants are left in place until the following spring.

Tips

Forget-me-not can be used in the front of flowerbeds or to edge beds and borders, in mixed containers and in rock gardens and on rock walls. You can also mix it with naturalized spring-flowering bulbs. This plant thrives in cooler parts of the garden.

M. sylvatica (photos this page)

Recommended

M. sylvatica forms a low mound of basal clusters of leaves. Clusters of small blue or white flowers with yellow centres are held on narrow, fuzzy stems above the foliage. **Ball series** has flowers in several colours. **'Victoria Blue'** produces 15–20 cm (6–8") mounds of foliage, covered by true blue flowers.

Problems & Pests

Slugs and snails, downy mildew, powdery mildew and rust may cause occasional trouble.

Fountain Grass

Pennisetum

Height: 60 cm –1.8 m (2–6') **Spread:** 45 cm –1.2 m (1½'–4') **Flower colour:** tan, gold flower spikes change to dark purple seedheads; attractive foliage

GRASSES ADD VARIETY AND INTEREST TO MANY TYPES OF LANDSCAPES and gardens, including water, rock, ecoscape and naturalized, Japanese, formal and container gardens. Ornamental grasses add movement, sound and colour year-round. They're best left intact from one season to the next so you can experience them as every subtle change takes place throughout the year, but especially in winter. Fluffy plumes poking through snowdrifts are a visual treat for us in the depths of winter, and they serve as forage for wildlife. An excellent assortment of annual and perennial grasses are available to choose from, each offering a touch of elegance to every style of garden.

Planting

Seeding: Direct sow outdoors once soil has warmed; indoors 2–3 weeks prior to last spring frost

Planting out: After last frost, once soil has warmed

Spacing: 25–30 cm (10–12")

Growing

Fountain grass grows best in **full sun** in **light, well-drained, moderately fertile** soil.

Tips

It can be used in beds and borders, massed, as a specimen or accent plant, or in the rock garden. It also works beautifully in containers as a replacement for dracaena or spikes.

Fountain grass can be dug up and brought inside and stored in a cool room for winter, or if grown in a container, cut back the foliage in fall and store the whole container. Make sure the root mass remains moist. The seeds produced by this plant are sterile, and the plant must be propagated vegetatively.

Recommended

P. glaucum **'Purple Majesty'** (purple majesty millet, ornamental millet) grows vigorously to 1.2–1.5 m (4–5') heights. Young plants are green-leaved, but as they mature, exposure to direct sunlight stimulates development of purple leaf colour. The entire plant then transforms to a deep, dark mahogany purple from base to tip. Tall bottle-brush stalks emerge from the stem with tan to gold flowers. Rich, deep purple seeds follow after the flowers and remain until hard frost.

P. setaceum 'Rubrum' (above)
P. glaucum 'Purple Majesty' (below)

P. setaceum **'Rubrum'** ('*Purpureum,*' fountain grass) is a dense, mound-forming, tender perennial grass that grows 90 cm–1.5 m (3–5') tall and 45–90 cm (18–36") wide. It has narrow, dark purple foliage and large, showy, rose-red flower spikes from mid-summer to fall. **'Burgundy Giant'** is a large plant that grows 1.8 m (6') tall and 60 cm–1.2 m (2–4') wide. The foliage is wider and coloured deep burgundy purple. Its nodding flower spikes are pinkish purple and grow up to 38 cm (15") long.

Four-O'Clock Flower

Mirabilis

Height: 45–90 cm (18–36") **Spread:** 45–60 cm (18–24") **Flower colour:** red, pink, magenta, yellow, white or bicoloured

FOUR-O'CLOCK FLOWER'S MOST INTERESTING ATTRIBUTE IS THE time of day when its flowers open. While it may not happen at four o'clock on the button, the flowers are known to open in the late afternoon, the opposite of morning glory and sundrops but similar to moonflower and evening primrose. Conversely, four o'clock flowers are also known to open on overcast and rainy afternoons—unlike the sun-worshipping gazania— just to be rebellious if nothing else. For those interested in theme gardens, four o'clock flower is a great choice for a night-blooming garden. Just remember to plant it close to a bedroom window or patio where its heavenly fragrance can be taken in and appreciated. *Mirabilis* is Latin for wonderful. Need we say more?

Planting

Seeding: Indoors in late winter; direct sow in mid-spring

Planting out: Mid-spring

Spacing: 40–60 cm (16–24")

Growing

Four-o'clock flower prefers **full sun** but tolerates partial shade. The soil should be **fertile,** though any **well-drained** soil is tolerated. This plant grows well in moist soil, but it is heat and drought tolerant.

Four-o'clock flower is a perennial treated as an annual, and it may be grown from its tuberous roots. Dig up the roots in fall, store them in a cool, dry place and replant them in spring to enjoy larger plants.

All parts of four-o'clock flower are poisonous, including the large black seeds. Considering the current trend of eating flowers, it is important that this plant be on the "do not eat" list.

Tips

Four-o'clock flower can be used in beds, borders, containers and window boxes. The flowers are scented, so the plant is often located near deck patios or terraces, where the scent can be enjoyed in the afternoon and evening.

Recommended

M. jalapa forms a bushy mound of foliage. The flowers may be solid or bicoloured. A single plant may bear flowers of several colours. **'Broken Colours'** produces solid or bicoloured, marbled or flecked flowers in vibrant combinations of yellow, magenta, pink and white. The colourful flowers are fragrant

M. jalapa (photos this page)

and produced on 50 cm (20") tall plants. **'Marvel of Peru,'** listed sometimes as a common name and other times as a cultivar, features the multi-coloured blooms that four-o'clock flower is known for. **'Red Glow'** bears brilliant red flowers. **Tea Time Series** bears a single flower colour on each plant. Flowers may be red, white or pink.

Problems & Pests

This plant has very few problems as long as it is given well-drained soil.

Fuchsia

Fuchsia

Height: 15–90 cm (6–36") **Spread:** 15–90 cm (6–36") **Flower colour:** pink, orange, red, purple, white; often bicoloured

FUCHSIA BLOSSOMS ARE REMINISCENT OF BALLERINAS, BALANCED on point, in exquisite costumes twirling around for all who adore them. In some parts of the world, fuchsia is known as "lady's eardrops" because the blossoms resemble dangly earrings. This annual bedding plant has adorned our gardens for decades and will likely never lose its place in our hearts. It's one of the most common annuals on the prairies and for reasons other than its sheer beauty. Once thought of as fussy and hard to take care of, fuchsias are very easy to grow and add visual flare to the garden. Often found in hanging baskets, they are one of the few prolific bloomers that prefers a shady location.

Some gardeners who have kept fuchsias over several years have trained the plants to adopt a tree form.

Planting

Seeding: Not recommended

Planting out: After last frost

Spacing: 30–60 cm (12–24")

Growing

Fuchsias are grown in **partial** or **light shade**. They generally do not tolerate summer heat, and full sun can be too hot for them. The soil should be **fertile, moist** and **well drained**. Fuchsias need to be watered well, particularly in hot weather.

The plants can develop rot problems in soggy soil, so ensure that the soil has good drainage. Fuchsias planted in well-aerated soil with plenty of perlite are almost impossible to over-water. As summer wears on, increase the amount of water given to container plants as the pots and baskets fill with thirsty roots. Fuchsias bloom on new growth, which will be stimulated by a high-nitrogen plant food.

Some fuchsias can be started from seed, although the germination rate can be poor and erratic. If you are up for the challenge, start the plants

'Winston Churchill' (above)
F. x *hybrida* cultivar (below)

Children, and some adults, enjoy popping the fat buds of fuchsias. The temptation to squeeze them is almost irresistible.

'Gartenmeister Bonstedt' (above)
'Snowburner' (below)

indoors in mid-winter. Ensure that the soil is warm, 20°–23.5° C (68°–75° F). Seeds can take from two weeks to two months to sprout. It may be late summer, or even the following summer, before you see any floral reward for your efforts.

Although fuchsias are difficult to start from seed, they are easy to propagate from cuttings. Snip off 15 cm (6") of new tip growth, remove the leaves from the lower third of the stem and insert the cuttings into soft soil or perlite. Once rooted and potted, the plants will bloom all summer.

Tips

Upright fuchsias can be used in mixed planters, beds and borders. The pendulous fuchsias are most often used in hanging baskets, but the flowers dangling from flexible branches also make attractive additions to planters and rock gardens.

Fuchsias should be deadheaded. Pluck the swollen seedpods from behind the fading petals or the seeds will ripen, robbing the plant of energy needed to produce flowers.

Fuchsias are perennials that are grown as annuals. To store them over winter, cut back the plants to 15 cm (6") stumps after the first light frost and place them in a dark, cold, but not freezing, location. Water just enough to keep the soil barely moist and do not feed. In mid-spring, repot the naked stumps, set them near a bright window and fertilize them lightly. Set your over-wintered plants outdoors after all danger of frost has passed.

Recommended

Fuchsia hybrids include hundreds of
cultivars and hybrids; just a few
examples are given here. The upright
fuchsias grow 45–90 cm (18–36")
tall, and the pendulous fuchsias
grow 15–60 cm (6–24") tall. Many
of the available hybrids cannot be
started from seed. **'Deep Purple'**
has purple petals and white sepals.
'Florabelle' is a good choice for
starting from seed because the
plants grow quickly to flowering
size. Its flowers are red and purple.
The Triphylla hybrid **'Gartenmeister
Bonstedt'** is an upright, shrubby
cultivar that grows about 60 cm
(24") tall and bears tubular, orange-
red flowers. The foliage is bronzy
red with purple undersides. **'Snowburner'** has white petals and pink
sepals. **'Swingtime'** has white petals
with pink bases and pink sepals.
This plant grows 30–60 cm (12–24")
tall, spreads about 15 cm (6") and
can be grown in a hanging basket or
as a relaxed upright plant in beds
and borders. **'Winston Churchill'**

has purple petals and pink sepals. It
grows 20–75 cm (8–30") tall, with an
equal spread. It is upright in form but
is often grown in hanging baskets.

Problems & Pests

Aphids, spider mites and whiteflies
are common insect pests. Diseases
such as crown rot, root rot and rust
can be avoided with good air circulation and drainage.

'Deep Purple' (below)

Gaura
Gaura

Height: 60 cm –1.2 m (24"–4') **Spread:** 60–90 cm (24–36")
Flower colour: white, pink; attractive foliage

TOUTED AS A PLANT FOR HOT CLIMATES AND DRY SOILS, GAURA
is perfectly suited to areas located in the scorching afternoon sun or in soil
that is less than perfect. Gaura may not be the flashiest flower in the garden,
but it is durable and dependable. The flowers attract butterflies, various
pollinating insects and bees, hence its other common name, bee blossom.
The airy appearance of the flowers balanced atop tall, wiry stems and the
delicate foliage are a great contrast against bold-leaved plants both in the
garden and on the patio in containers, where the butterflies can be most
appreciated.

Planting

Seeding: Start seed indoors in early spring

Planting out: Spring

Spacing: 45–60 cm (18–24")

All 20 species of Gaura
*are native to North
America.*

Growing

Gaura prefers **full sun** but tolerates partial shade. The soil should be **fertile, moist** and **well drained**. Gaura is drought tolerant once it is established. Most plants self-seed, and the new seedlings can be carefully transplanted if desired.

Tips

Gaura makes a wonderful addition to mixed borders. Its airy habit softens the effect of brightly coloured flowers. It bears only a few flowers at a time, but if the faded flower spikes are removed it will keep flowering all summer. Plant gaura behind low, bushy plants such as hardy geraniums, cornflowers or asters to display the delicate, floating flowers to best advantage. Gaura also works well in containers as a subtle accent to bolder-leaved plants.

Recommended

G. x **'Karalee Petite Pink'** bears bright pink, orchid-like, spurred flowers. Wiry flower stems tower high above the fine, sparse dark green to burgundy foliage. This hybrid grows 25–35 cm (10–14") in height.

G. x **'Karalee White'** is very similar to its pink-flowering counterpart but has white flowers with a light hint of pink. The white flowers are slightly larger than the pink, but the overall plant is a little smaller.

G. lindheimeri (white gaura, Lindheimer's bee blossom) is a perennial we grow as an annual. It forms a large, bushy clump 60–75 cm (24–30") tall and 60–90 cm (24–36") wide. Spikes of small, white or pinkish flowers

G. lindheimeri

are borne on long, slender stems in summer and early fall. **'Corrie's Gold'** has a more compact habit, growing 60–90 cm (24–36") tall. It has yellow-variegated foliage and its white flowers are tinged with pink. **'Siskiyou Pink'** has bright pink flowers. **'Whirling Butterflies'** is a compact, long-flowering cultivar that grows 60–90 cm (24–36") tall. The white flowers are borne from late spring to early fall. This cultivar will not self-seed.

G. x **'Perky Pink'** is a new gaura from Australia that bears reddish coloured foliage and pink, mottled flowers. It is a compact hybrid that grows 20–30 cm (8–12").

Problems & Pests

Rare problems with rust, fungal leaf spot, downy mildew and powdery mildew can occur.

Gazania

Gazania

Height: usually 15–20 cm (6–8"); may reach 30–45 cm (12–18")
Spread: 20–30 cm (8–12") **Flower colour:** red, orange, yellow, pink, cream, white; attractive foliage

GAZANIA IS TRULY ONE OF THE MORE INTERESTING AND VISUALLY stunning annuals available. The flowers are beautifully decorated with fiery colours, both striped and solid, the perfect complement to the rough-looking, deeply lobed, coarsely textured foliage. There is really no application for which gazanias aren't suited. Whether it's their job to fill a container, to enhance a hanging basket or to adorn a mixed bed en masse, they'll never let you down. If gazanias have a fault, however, it's that they tend to hide their glorious little faces on overcast days by closing up tight, only to burst forth when the sun emerges from behind the clouds.

Planting

Seeding: Indoors in late winter; direct sow after last frost

Planting out: After last frost

Spacing: 15–25 cm (6–10")

Growing

Gazania grows best in **full sun** but tolerates some shade. The soil should be of **poor to average fertility, sandy** and **well drained**. Gazania grows best in weather over 26.5° C (80° F) and is drought tolerant.

Tips

Low-growing gazania makes an excellent groundcover and is also useful on exposed slopes, in mixed containers and as an edging in flowerbeds. It is a wonderful plant for a xeriscape or dry garden design.

Recommended

G. rigens forms a low basal rosette of lobed foliage. Large, daisy-like flowers with pointed petals are borne on strong stems above the plant. The petals often have a contrasting stripe or spot. The flowers tend to close on gloomy days and in low light. The species is rarely grown, but there are several hybrid cultivars available. **Daybreak Series** bears flowers in many colours, often with a contrasting stripe down the centre of each petal. These flowers will stay open

G. rigens Daybreak Series (above)
G. rigens cultivars (below)

on dull days but close on rainy or very dark days. **Kiss Series** has compact plants that bear large flowers in several colours. Seeds are available by individual flower colour or as a mix. **Mini-star Series** has compact plants and flowers in many colours with a contrasting dot at the base of each petal. **Sundance Mix** bears flowers in reds and yellows with dark, contrasting stripes down the centres of the petals.

Problems & Pests

Overwatering is the likely cause of any problems encountered by gazania.

Geranium

Pelargonium

Height: 20 cm –1 m (8"–3') **Spread:** 15 cm –1.2 m (6"–4') **Flower colour:** red, pink, violet, orange, salmon, white, purple; attractive foliage

WHERE DOES ONE START WITH GERANIUMS EXCEPT TO SAY THAT they have been around for over 200 years and continue to surprise us. Every season, it seems, there are new selections to choose from. Although the classic geraniums are here to stay, recent introductions have cast a whole new light on this beloved group of annuals. The new forms, colours and combinations of ornate flowers and foliage are very exciting. Take the new Fireworks Collection, for example, a hot new series of geraniums bearing starry-shaped flowers in tightly packed clusters, exhibiting bright, vivid colours. Even the foliage has been transformed from the classic round leaf to a maple-shaped leaf. We dare you to pass by the geranium aisle now!

Planting

Seeding: Indoors in early winter

Planting out: After last frost

Spacing: Zonal geranium, about 30 cm (12"); ivy-leaved geranium, 60–90 cm (24–36"); scented geraniums, 30–90 cm (12–36")

Growing

Geraniums prefer **full sun** but tolerate partial shade, although they may not bloom as profusely. The soil should be **fertile** and **well drained**.

Geraniums are slow to grow from seed, so purchasing plants may prove easier. However, if you would like to try starting your own from seed, start them indoors in early winter and cover them with clear plastic to maintain humidity until they germinate. Once the seedlings have three or four leaves, transplant them into individual 7.5–10 cm (3–4") pots. Keep your transplants in bright locations because they need lots of light to maintain their compact shape.

Deadheading is essential to keep geraniums blooming and looking neat. The flowerheads are attached to long stems that break off easily where they attach to the plant. Some gardeners prefer to snip off just the flowering end in order to avoid potentially damaging the plant's stem.

Tips

Use zonal geranium in beds, borders and containers. Ivy-leaved geraniums are mostly used in hanging baskets and containers but can also be grouped together to form a bushy, spreading groundcover.

P. peltatum cultivar (above), *P. zonale* cultivar (below)

Geraniums are tender perennials from South Africa that are treated as annuals. They can be kept indoors over winter in a bright room.

Recommended

***P.* hybrids** include a great many combinations of flower and leaf colour, shape and overall form. Fancy leaf geraniums are incredibly popular in the market and for good reason. Plants in the **Illusion Collection** are similar in appearance to traditional geranium hybrids but unique in

P. odoratissimum (apple-scented geranium)

their cultural requirements. Ordinarily geraniums are sun worshippers, but **Illusion Cherry Rose, Orange, Pink** and **Violet** are shade-flowering hybrids. The flower colours are vibrant enough to brighten a shady corner and grow 25–38 cm (10–15") tall. Another fancy-leaf, sun-loving hybrid is **'Lotusland,'** which bears single, finely cut magenta flowers and golden foliage with bronze centres;

P. scented geranium hybrid

'Vancouver Centennial' bears red wine–coloured leaves edged in gold and star-shaped scarlet orange flowers.

P. peltatum (ivy-leaved geranium) grows up to 30 cm (12") tall and up to 1.2 m (4') wide. Many colours are available. Plants in the **Summer Showers Series** can take four or more months to flower from seed. **Tornado Series** is very good for hanging baskets and containers. The plants are quite compact, and the flowers are either lilac or white.

***P.* species and cultivars** (scented geraniums, scented pelargoniums) is a large group of geraniums that have scented leaves. The scents are grouped into the categories of rose, mint, citrus, fruit, spice and pungent. In the following list, a parent of each cultivar is indicated in parentheses. Some cultivars, such as **'Apple'** (*P. odoratissimum*), readily self-seed and stay true to form, but most must be propagated by cuttings to retain their ornamental and fragrant qualities. Many cultivars have variegated leaves. Intensely scented cultivars include **'Chocolate-Mint'** (*P. quercifolium*), **'Lemon'** (*P. crispum*), **'Nutmeg'** (*P.* x *fragrans*), **'Old-fashioned Rose'** (*P. graveolens*), **'Peppermint'** (*P. tomentosum*), **'Prince Rupert'** (*P. crispum*), **'Rober's Lemon Rose'** (*P. graveolens*) and **'Strawberry'** (*P.* x *scarboroviae*).

P. zonale (zonal geranium) grows up to 60 cm (24") tall and 30 cm (12") wide. Dwarf varieties grow up to 20 cm (8") tall and 15 cm (6") wide. The flowers are red, pink, purple, orange or white. Many of the zonal geraniums have contrasting bands of colours on their leaves. These often have to be propagated by cuttings to retain those characteristics. The **Fireworks Collection** is a new series with ornate, maple-shaped leaves and finely cut flowers in cherry pink, pastel pink and salmon and bicolour combinations. **Orbit Series** has attractive, compact, early-blooming plants. The seed is often sold in a mixed packet, but some individual colours are available. **Pillar Series** includes upright plants that grow up to 90 cm (36") tall with staking. Salmon, violet and orange flowers are available. **Pinto Series** has flowers in all colours, and seed is generally sold by the colour so you don't have to purchase a mixed packet and hope you like the colours you get. Flowers in the **Ripple Series** are speckled with darker and lighter shades of the main colour. 'Raspberry Ripple' bears salmon pink flowers speckled with white and red streaks.

Problems & Pests

Aphids will flock to overfertilized plants, but they can usually be washed off before they do much damage. Leaf spot and blight may bother geraniums growing in cool, moist soil.

P. zonale Fireworks Collection (above)
P. peltatum cultivar (below)

Edema is an unusual condition to which geraniums are susceptible. This disease occurs when a plant is overwatered and absorbs so much of the water that the leaf cells burst. A warty surface develops on the leaves. It is more of a cosmetic problem because plants seem to continue to grow as long as the roots don't rot. There is no cure, although it can be avoided by watering carefully and removing any damaged leaves as the plant grows. The condition is more common in ivy-leaved geranium.

Globe Amaranth
Gomphrena

Height: 15–75 cm (6–30") **Spread:** 15–38 cm (6–15") **Flower colour:** purple, orange, magenta, pink, white, sometimes red

GLOBE AMARANTH IS WELL KNOWN TO FLORAL DESIGNERS AND crafters alike. It's the rest of the gardening population that needs the introduction. So let us have the honour of doing just that. Globe amaranth bears globular, colourful flowerheads that are all the rage in floral design and even more so for those who create unique, everlasting arrangements. The tightly packed, vivid flowers are known to hold their colour even when dried. In the garden, they're a little slow to bloom but are well worth the wait. The papery pompom flowers add colour to the garden for weeks in late summer and fall when most others are beginning to wane. Once they've completed their job for the growing season, and before first frost, cut them at the base, stripping the leaves from their stems. Bundle the stems together, gently bind them together with a string or elastic and hang them upside down in a warm, dry, well-ventilated area. Then let your imagination take off.

The clover-like heads actually consist of showy bracts (modified leaves) from which the tiny flowers emerge.

Planting

Seeding: Indoors in late winter

Planting out: After last frost

Spacing: 25 cm (10")

Growing

Globe amaranth prefers **full sun**. The soil should be of **average fertility** and **well drained**. This plant likes hot weather. It needs watering only when drought-like conditions persist. Seeds will germinate more quickly if soaked in water for two to four days before sowing. They need warm soil, above 21° C (70° F), to sprout.

The long-lasting flowers require only occasional deadheading.

G. globosa (photos this page); with nasturtium (above)

Tips

Use globe amaranth in an informal or cottage garden. This plant is often underused because it doesn't start flowering until later in summer than many other annuals. Don't overlook it—the blooms are worth the wait, and they provide colour from mid-summer until the first frost.

Recommended

G. globosa forms a rounded, bushy plant 30–60 cm (12–24") tall that is dotted with papery, clover-like flowers in purple, magenta, white or pink. **'Buddy'** is a more compact plant, 15–30 cm (6–12") tall, with deep purple flowers. **'Lavender Lady'** grows into a large plant, up to 60 cm (24") tall and bears lavender purple flowers.

***G.* 'Strawberry Fields'** is a hybrid with bright orange-red or red flowers.

It grows about 75 cm (30") tall and spreads about half as much.

Problems & Pests

Globe amaranth is susceptible to some fungal diseases, such as grey mold and leaf spot.

Godetia
Clarkia, Satin Flower
Clarkia (Godetia)

Height: 20 cm –1.2 m (8"–4') **Spread:** 25–30 cm (10–12")
Flower colour: pink, red, purple, white, some bicoloured

MY FIRST EXPERIENCE WITH GODETIA WAS IN VICTORIA, B.C., AT the Butchart Gardens many years ago. I remember thinking how unique and lovely the satiny flowers were, overflowing in massive window boxes in myriad colours. Once I learned a little more about godetia and its love of locations with cool summers, it occurred to me how well it would grow in Alberta. This old-fashioned annual has been a gardener's dream for generations, likely because it blooms so prolifically, is easily started from seed, isn't fussy about soil conditions and requires no special care. Stunning in the garden, the flowers are also ideal for fresh arrangements. Just make sure to cut the stems just as the buds are beginning to open to ensure a long blast of colour indoors.

Planting
Seeding: Direct sow in spring for summer bloom or in mid- to late summer for fall flowers
Spacing: 15 cm (6")

Growing

Godetias grow equally well in **full sun** or **light shade**. The soil should be **well drained, light, sandy** and of **poor** or **average fertility**. Fertilizer will promote leaf growth at the expense of flower production. These plants don't like to be overwatered, so water sparingly and be sure to let them dry out between waterings. They do best in the cool weather of spring and fall.

Starting seeds indoors is not recommended. Seed plants where you want them to grow because they are difficult to transplant. Thin seedlings to about 15 cm (6") apart.

Tips

Godetias are useful in beds, borders, containers and rock gardens. The flowers can be used in fresh arrangements. These plants flower quickly from seed, so direct sow in early spring to provide a show of satiny flowers before the hardier summer annuals steal the show.

A planting in mid- to late summer will provide flowers in fall.

Recommended

C. amoena (*Godetia amoena, G. grandiflora;* godetia, satin flower, farewell-to-spring) is a bushy, upright plant. It grows up to 75 cm (30") tall, spreads 30 cm (12") and bears clusters of ruffled, cup-shaped flowers in shades of pink, red, white and purple. **'Rembrandt'** bears semi-double, azalea-like flowers in pale pink, white and carmine blends. **Satin Series** has compact plants that grow 20–30 cm (8–12") tall. The single flowers come in

C. amoena (above), *C. unguiculata* (below)

many colours, including some bicolours.

C. unguiculata (*C. elegans;* clarkia, Rocky Mountain garland flower) is a tall, branching plant that grows 30–1.2 m (1–4') high and spreads up to 25 cm (10"). Its small, ruffled flowers can be pink, purple, red or white. **'Apple Blossom'** bears apricot pink double flowers. **'Royal Bouquet'** bears very ruffled double flowers in pink, red or light purple.

Problems & Pests

Root rot can occur if the soil is poorly drained.

Heliotrope
Cherry Pie Plant
Heliotropium

Height: 20 cm–1.2 m (8"–4')-**Spread:** 30–60 cm (12–24")
Flower colour: purple, blue, white; attractive foliage

HELIOTROPE WAS INTRODUCED INTO CULTIVATION IN EUROPE IN 1757, and by the 19th century, it was used extensively in gardens all over the world. It was nicknamed the "cherry pie plant" because the fragrance produced by the rich purple flowers is reminiscent of freshly baked cherry pie. That fragrance is often used as a note in perfumes even today. The scent has also been compared to vanilla, almond and baby powder. Even for the scent-challenged, heliotrope is a must-have plant and a striking contrast to many flowers, especially those with warmer colours. The end result is one colour playing off another, bringing all of heliotrope's best attributes forward for all to enjoy.

Planting
Seeding: Indoors in mid-winter

Planting out: Once soil has warmed

Spacing: 30–45 cm (12–18")

Growing

Heliotrope grows best in **full sun**. The soil should be **fertile, rich in organic matter, moist** and **well drained**. Although overwatering will kill heliotrope, if left to dry to the point of wilting, the plant will be slow to recover.

Heliotrope is sensitive to cold weather, so plant it out after all danger of frost has passed. Protect plants with newspaper or a floating row cover (available at garden centres) if an unexpected late frost or cold snap should arrive. Container-grown plants can be brought indoors at night if frost is expected.

H. arborescens

Tips

Heliotrope is ideal for growing in containers or beds near windows and patios where the wonderful scent of the flowers can be enjoyed.

This plant can be pinched and shaped. Create a tree form, or standard, by pinching off the lower branches as the plant grows until it reaches the height you desire; then pinch the top to encourage the plant to bush out. A shorter, bushy form is also popular and can be created by pinching all the tips that develop to encourage the plant to bush out at ground level.

Heliotrope can be grown indoors as a houseplant in a sunny window. A plant may survive for years if kept outdoors all summer and indoors all winter in a cool, bright room.

Recommended

H. arborescens is a low, bushy shrub that is treated as an annual. It grows 45–60 cm (18–24") tall, with an equal spread. Large clusters of purple, blue or white, scented flowers are produced all summer. Some new cultivars are not as strongly scented as the species. **'Alba'** is a white variety with a strong, heady scent and **'Atlantic'** produces deep purple-blue, vanilla-scented flower clusters. **'Black Beauty'** has deep, dark flowers and **'Blue Wonder,'** is a compact plant that was developed for heavily scented flowers. Plants grow up to 40 cm (16") tall with dark purple flowers. **'Dwarf Marine'** ('Mini Marine') is a compact, bushy plant with fragrant, purple flowers. It grows 20–30 cm (8–12") tall and also makes a good houseplant for a bright location. **'Fragrant Delight'** is an older culti-var with royal purple, intensely fragrant flowers. It can reach a height of 1.2 m (4') if grown as a standard. **'Marine'** has violet blue flowers and grows about 45 cm (18") tall.

Problems & Pests

Aphids and whiteflies can be problems.

Hollyhock

Alcea

Height: 1.5–2.5 m (5–8') **Spread:** 60 cm (24") **Flower colour:** yellow, white, apricot, pink, red, purple, reddish black; attractive foliage

HOLLYHOCKS MAKE A STRONG VERTICAL STATEMENT IN the garden and are very impressive, both in height and colour. This traditional English garden favourite loves the prairie climate, soil conditions and bright sunny skies. Each individual, single flower is similar in many ways to its relatives in the mallow family, *Malvaceae*, including hibiscus, lavatera, flowering maple and mallow. The family itself is made up of over 1500 species of plants, so the appeal is universal. As generations have before us, plant hollyhocks in locations with a little shelter from the wind or plan on providing some type of support. Otherwise, they require little in order to shine.

Planting

Seeding: Start indoors in mid-winter

Planting out: After last frost

Spacing: 45–60 cm (18–24")

The powdered roots of plants in the mallow family, to which hollyhocks belong, were once used to make soft lozenges to soothe sore throats. Though still popular around the campfire, marshmallows no longer contain the throat-soothing properties they originally had.

Growing

Hollyhocks prefer **full sun** but tolerate partial shade. The soil should be **average to rich** and **well drained**.

Plant hollyhocks in a different part of the garden each year to keep hollyhock rust at bay.

Tips

Because they are so tall, hollyhocks look best at the back of the border or in the centre of an island bed. In a windy location they will need to be staked. Plant them against a fence or wall for support.

If the main stem is pinched out early in the season, hollyhocks will be shorter and bushier with smaller flower spikes. These shorter stems are less likely to be broken by wind and can be left unstaked.

Old-fashioned types typically have single flowers, and they grow much taller and are more disease resistant than newer hybrids.

Recommended

A. rosea forms a rosette of basal leaves; the tall, flowering stalk develops ruffled single or double blooms. **'Chater's Double'** bears double flowers in a wide range of colours. **'Nigra'** bears reddish black single flowers with yellow centres. **'Summer Carnival'** bears double flowers in yellows and reds. It blooms in early summer and produces flowers lower on the stem than the other cultivars.

A. rugosa (Russian Hollyhock) is similar to *A. rosea* but is more resistant to hollyhock rust. It bears pale yellow to orangy yellow, single flowers.

A. rosea 'Nigra' (above), *A. rosea* cultivars (below)

Problems & Pests

Hollyhock rust is the biggest problem. These plants are also susceptible to bacterial and fungal leaf spot. Slugs and cutworms occasionally attack young growth. Sometimes mallow flea beetles, aphids or Japanese beetles cause trouble.

Hyacinth Bean
Egyptian Bean, Lablab Bean
Lablab (Dolichos)

Height: 3–4.5 m (10–15') **Spread:** variable **Flower colour:** purple, white; also grown for purple pods and foliage

HYACINTH BEAN, SIMILAR TO OTHER ANNUAL VINES, IS ON A MISSION and that mission is to grow to great heights and spreads, produce heaps of flowers and sometimes fruit along the way in three months flat. This is a very important quality with our relatively short season here in Alberta. The foliage is lush and provides a density that beats most other annual vines hands down. This plant is ideal for structures or views that you're trying to disguise for the summer months. The flowers are an added benefit, and they're followed by colourful fruit. Hummingbirds love the little sweet pea-like flowers.

Planting

Seeding: Direct sow around last frost date, or start indoors in peat pots in early spring

Planting out: After last frost

Spacing: 30–45 cm (12–18")

Growing

Hyacinth bean prefers **full sun**. The soil should be **fertile, moist** and **well drained**.

Tips

Hyacinth bean needs a trellis, net, pole or other structure to twine up. Plant it against a fence or near a balcony. If you grow it as a ground-cover, make sure it doesn't engulf smaller plants.

L. purpureus (photos this page)

Recommended

L. purpureus (*Dolichos lablab*) is a vigorous twining vine. It can grow up to 9 m (30') tall, but when grown as an annual it grows about 3–4.5 m (10–15') tall. It bears many purple or white flowers over the summer, followed by deep purple pods. **'Giganteus'** has large, white flowers and **'Ruby Moon'** bears bicoloured pink and dark purple fragrant flowers that later turn into large brown seedpods. The foliage is deep green and purple-brown.

Problems & Pests

Rare problems with leaf spot can occur.

The purple pods are edible if thoroughly cooked with two to four changes of water. Try adding the cooked beans to a stir-fry to add some unusual colour.

Ice Plant
Livingstone Daisy
Dorotheanthus

Height: 15 cm (6") **Spread:** 30 cm (12") **Flower colour:** pink, white, purple, crimson, orange, yellow or bicoloured; unique foliage

THE BRIGHTLY COLOURED, DAISY-LIKE FLOWERS AREN'T THE ONLY eye-catching characteristic of this annual. If you look closely at the leaves under the flowers you will see little spots or bumps that resemble ice crystals. Ice plant's dramatic colours give it a unique appearance. It's right at home with other succulents like perennial sedums, hens and chicks and portulaca, as all enjoy sun and dry conditions. Ice plant is the perfect filler in a location with other low-growing, sun-loving plants, especially perennials. They will add a spark of excitement between perennial bloom periods, never allowing for a moment without colour.

Planting

Seeding: Indoors in late winter; direct sow in spring

Planting out: After last frost

Spacing: 30 cm (12")

Growing

Ice plant likes to grow in **full sun**. The soil should be of **poor to average fertility, sandy** and **well drained**.

Tips

Brightly flowered and low growing, ice plant can be used along edges of borders, on dry slopes, in rock gardens or in mixed containers. It can also be used between the stones of a walkway or around the edges of a paved patio.

The flowers close on cloudy days.

Recommended

D. bellidiformis (*Mesembryanthemum criniflorum*) is a low-growing, spreading plant. It bears brightly coloured, daisy-like flowers. **'Lunette'** ('Yellow Ice') bears bright yellow flowers with red centres. **Magic Carpet Series** has flowers in shades of purple, pink, white, yellow or orange. The petal bases are often lighter in colour than the tips.

Problems & Pests

Slugs, snails and aphids may be troublesome.

D. bellidiformis (above), 'Lunette' (below)

The common name ice plant refers to the tiny crystals that form on the leaves.

Impatiens
Busy Lizzie, Touch-me-not
Impatiens

Height: 15–90 cm (6–36") **Spread:** 30–60 cm (12–24") **Flower colour:** shades of purple, red, burgundy, pink, yellow, orange, apricot, white or bicoloured; attractive foliage

FOR MANY, MANY YEARS, PRAIRIE GARDENERS HAD LITTLE OTHER than impatiens to add colour to their shade beds. There are a wide variety of shade options these days, but few even come close to impatiens. Impatiens are an old-fashioned group of annuals that adore shade and are guaranteed to brighten up the darkest of corners. They grow vigorously, producing copious amounts of flowers nonstop from spring to fall. Each type of impatiens has another planting application, leaving most gardeners looking for an excuse to plant more. Although there have been few new, innovative selections on the market lately, you're guaranteed to succeed with traditional impatiens varieties.

Planting

Seeding: Indoors in mid-winter; balsam impatiens indoors in late winter

Planting out: Once soil has warmed

Spacing: 30–45 cm (12–18")

Growing

All impatiens do best in **partial shade** or **light shade** but tolerate full shade or, if kept moist, full sun. Of the various impatiens, New Guinea impatiens and balsam impatiens are the best adapted to sunny locations. The soil should be **fertile, humus rich, moist** and **well drained**. Though it is a heavy feeder, New Guinea impatiens does not like wet feet, so good drainage is a must.

Don't cover the seeds—they germinate best when exposed to light.

Tips

Impatiens is known for its ability to grow and flower profusely even in deep shade. Mass plant it in beds under trees, along shady fences or

I. walleriana (photos this page)

walls or in porch planters. It also looks lovely in hanging baskets. The new double-flowering varieties work beautifully as accent plants in hosta and wildflower gardens.

New Guinea impatiens is almost shrubby in form and is popular in patio planters, beds and borders. It grows well in full sun and may not flower as profusely in deep shade.

I. balsamina (above), *I. hawkeri* (below)

This plant is grown as much for its variegated leaves as for its flowers.

Balsam impatiens was popular in the Victorian era and has recently experienced a comeback in popularity. This plant is more upright than the other two impatiens and is attractive when grouped in beds and borders.

Recommended

New impatiens varieties are introduced every year, expanding the selection of sizes, forms and colours. The following list includes varieties that are popular year after year.

I. balsamina (balsam impatiens) grows 30–90 cm (12–36") tall and up to 45 cm (18") wide. The flowers come in shades of purple, red, pink or white. There are several double-flowered cultivars, such as **'Camellia-flowered,'** with pink, red or white flowers on plants up to 60 cm (24") tall; **'Tom Thumb,'** with pink, red, purple or white flowers on plants to 30 cm (12") tall; and **'Topknot,'** with large flowers in a similar range of colours held above the foliage on plants 30 cm (12") tall.

I. hawkeri (New Guinea hybrids; New Guinea impatiens) grows 30–60 cm (12–24") tall and 30 cm (12") wide or wider. The flowers come in shades of red, orange, pink, purple or white. The foliage is often variegated with a yellow stripe down the centre of each leaf. **'Java'** has bronzed leaves and flowers in lavender, salmon, pink or white. This cultivar can be grown from seed. **'Tango'** can also be grown from seed. This compact plant grows 30–45 cm (12–18") tall and wide and has orange flowers.

I. **Seashell Series** is a new group of African hybrids with flowers in shades of yellow, orange, apricot and pink. Plants grow 20–25 cm (8–10") tall and spread about 30 cm (12").

I. walleriana (impatiens, busy Lizzie) grows 15–45 cm (6–18") tall and up to 60 cm (24") wide. The flowers come in shades of red, orange, pink, purple or white, or are bicoloured. **Elfin Series** is a common group of cultivars. The flowers are available in many shades, including bicolours. The compact plants grow about 30 cm (12") tall, but they may spread more. **Fiesta Series** plants grow about 30 cm (12") tall, with an equal spread, and bear double flowers in shades of pink, orange, red and burgundy. With their habit and flower form, they resemble small rose bushes. **Mosaic Series** has uniquely coloured flowers, with the margins and most of the petals speckled in a darker shade of the petal colour. **Tempo Series** has a wide range of colours, including bicolours, and flowers with contrasting margins on the petals. **'Victoria Rose'** is an award-winning cultivar, with deep pink, double or semi-double flowers.

Problems & Pests
Fungal leaf spot, stem rot, *Verticillium* wilt, whiteflies and aphids can cause trouble.

With their reliable blooming in shade, and their wide variety of colours and types, impatiens are America's top-selling bedding plants.

I. hawkeri (above), *I. walleriana* (below)

Lantana
Shrub Verbena
Lantana

Height: 45–60 cm (18–24") **Spread:** up to 1.2 m (4') **Flower colour:** yellow, orange, pink, purple, red, white, often in combination; attractive foliage

GARDENERS ARE ALWAYS ON THE LOOKOUT FOR PEST-FREE PLANTS that are easy to care for and that take the heat. Lantana is such a plant. This annual bedding plant performs best in full sun, providing wave after wave of brightly coloured flowers and coarsely textured, fragrant foliage. Lantana isn't only attractive to prairie gardeners, it is also loved by butterflies. The same can be said for verbena, a close relative. The two plants are great garden companions and blend beautifully with cosmos, calendula and geraniums.

It's not uncommon to find standard tree form lantana specimens. They're easy to create over time, with careful pruning and the right conditions, because of their woody stems.

Planting

Seeding: Start seed indoors in spring; soil temperature 16°–17.5° C (61°–64° F)

Planting out: Into warm soil after danger of frost has passed

Spacing: 60 cm–1.2 m (2–4')

Growing

Lantana grows best in **full sun** but tolerates partial shade. The soil should be **fertile, moist** and **well drained**, but the plant can handle heat and drought.

If you would like to start plants for the following summer but don't want to store a large plant over winter, take cuttings in late summer.

Tips

Lantana is a tender shrub that is grown as an annual. It is useful in beds and borders as well as in mixed containers and hanging baskets.

All parts may cause discomfort if ingested and contact with foliage may irritate sensitive skin.

'Red Spread' (above), 'New Gold' (below)

Recommended

L. camara is a bushy plant that bears round clusters of flowers in many colours. **'Feston Rose'** has flowers that open yellow and mature to bright pink. **'New Gold'** bears clusters of bright yellow flowers. **'Radiation'** has flowers that open yellow and mature to red. **'Red Spread'** produces a mound of tightly packed foliage and a profuse showing of red flower clusters.

Problems & Pests

Rust, spider mites, stem rot and leaf spot are all possibilities.

Larkspur
Rocket Larkspur, Annual Delphinium
Consolida (Delphinium)

Height: 30 cm–1.2 m (1–4') **Spread:** 15–35 cm (6–14") **Flower colour:** blue, purple, pink, white

LARKSPUR IS A WONDERFUL ADDITION TO THE GARDEN AND IS very easy to grow. Simply sprinkle larkspur seeds in a sunny location, and voilà! In no time at all, you'll enjoying beautiful muted shades of purples, pinks, white and blues. Mind you, these flowers aren't strictly for use outdoors. The tall flower stalks can be cut for fresh arrangements to enjoy in the house, and if you hang the stalks to dry, they are ideal for everlasting arrangements. The colours hold fast and will not fade. Larkspur doesn't like to have its roots disturbed and should be transplanted only as a very young seedling.

Planting

Seeding: Indoors in midwinter; direct sow in early or mid-spring, as soon as soil can be worked

Planting out: Mid-spring

Spacing: 30 cm (12")

Growing

Larkspur does equally well in **full sun** or **light shade**. The soil should be **fertile, rich in organic matter** and **well drained**. Keep the roots cool and add a light mulch; dried grass clippings or shredded leaves work well. Don't put mulch too close to the base of the plant, or crown rot may develop. Another option is to plant larkspurs close together so that the centres of plants are only 15–20 cm (6–8") apart. Then the upper portion of the plants will shade the roots, so you will not need to use mulch.

Plant seeds in peat pots to prevent roots from being damaged when the plants are transplanted. Seeds started indoors may benefit from being chilled in the refrigerator for one week prior to sowing. Mix seeds in a plastic bag with moist peat moss or sand before placing them in-the refrigerator.

Deadhead to keep larkspur blooming well into fall. Larkspur will self-sow, giving you more of these lovely plants to share.

Tips

Plant groups of larkspur in mixed borders or cottage gardens. The tallest varieties may require staking to stay upright.

Recommended

C. ajacis (*C. ambigua, D. ajacis*) is an upright plant with feathery foliage. It bears spikes of purple, blue, pink or white flowers. **Dwarf Rocket Series** includes plants that grow 30–50 cm (12–20") tall and 15–25 cm (6–10") wide and bloom

C. ajacis

in many colours. **'Earl Grey'** grows 90 cm–1.2 m (3–4') tall and bears flowers in an intriguing colour between slate grey and gunmetal grey. **'Frosted Skies'** grows to 45 cm (18") and bears large, semi-double flowers in a beautiful bicolour of blue and white. **Giant Imperial Series** has plants that grow 60–90 cm (24–36") tall and up to 35 cm (14") wide and come in many colours.

Problems & Pests

Slugs and snails are potential problems. Powdery mildew and crown or root rot are avoidable if you water thoroughly, but not too often, and ensure good air circulation.

Lavatera
Mallow
Lavatera

Height: 50 cm–3 m (20"–10') **Spread:** 45 cm–1.5 m (18"–5')
Flower colour: pink, salmon, white, red, purple; attractive foliage

LAVATERA HAS A TENDENCY TO OUTLIVE ITS SPACE AND ENCROACH
on other plants, so be careful where you sow it. Its taproot is very long, and
if you do not remove the taproot entirely, it will just continue to grow.
Lavatera is a prolific bloomer, however, and is well worth having in your
garden. It has an airy look about it and is useful for providing late
summer and fall colour. Lavatera thrives in our climate, with our
cool nights and warm days, and it is the perfect substitute for
plants like hibiscus, as the flowers are very similar in appearance.

Planting

Seeding: Indoors in late winter; direct sow
in spring

Planting out: After last frost

Spacing: 45–60 cm
(18–24")

Growing

Lavatera prefers **full sun**. The soil should be of **average fertility, light** and **well drained**. These plants like cool, moist weather and may not flower much until the nights begin to cool in late summer. Select a site where the plants will be protected from strong winds.

These plants resent having their roots disturbed when they are transplanted and tend to do better when sown directly in the garden. If starting seeds indoors, use peat pots.

Tips

Lavatera plants can be used as colourful backdrops behind smaller plants in a bed or border. The blooms make attractive cut flowers and are edible.

Lavateras grow to be fairly large and shrubby. Stake tall varieties to keep them from falling over in summer rain showers.

Recommended

L. arborea (tree mallow) is a large plant, capable of growing 3 m (10') tall and spreading 1.5 m (5'). The funnel-shaped flowers are pinkish purple. The lifespan of this plant is undetermined. Typically grown as an annual, it can sometimes be treated as a biennial or perennial. The cultivar **'Variegata'** has cream-mottled leaves.

L. cachemiriana has light pink flowers. It can grow up to 2.4 m (8') tall and is usually half as wide. As the scientific name indicates, this plant is native to Kashmir.

L. trimestris 'Mont Blanc' (above)
L. trimestris 'Silver Cup' (below)

L. trimestris is a bushy plant up to 1.2 m (4') tall and 45–60 cm (18–24") in spread. It bears red, pink or white, funnel-shaped flowers. **Beauty Series** has plants in a variety of colours. **'Mont Blanc'** bears white flowers on compact plants that grow to about 50 cm (20") tall. **'Silver Cup'** has cup-shaped, light pink flowers with dark pink veins.

Problems & Pests

Plant lavateras in well-drained soil to avoid root rot. Destroy any rust-infected plants.

Licorice Plant
False Licorice
Helichrysum

Height: 50 cm (20") **Spread:** about 90 cm (36"); sometimes up to 1.8 m (6') **Flower colour:** yellow-white; plant grown for foliage

LICORICE PLANT IS AN ELEGANT AND SUBDUED ADDITION TO decorative containers and planters, especially those filled with plants in shades of grey. The soft, grey, fuzzy leaves mix beautifully with contrasting and vivid foliage and flowers as well. Monochromatic garden schemes are all the rage, and licorice plant is ideal for this type of design. It's not hard to find a myriad of grey- and silver-leaved plants these days and they often prefer similar conditions. A container filled with licorice plant, dusty miller, silver leaf gazanias, tricolour sage and various silvery grasses is guaranteed to boost the colour of surrounding plants.

Planting
Seeding: Not recommended
Planting out: After last frost
Spacing: About 75 cm (30")

Growing

Licorice plant prefers **full sun**. The soil should be of **poor to average fertility, neutral** or **alkaline** and **well drained**. Licorice plant wilts when the soil dries but revives quickly once watered. If it outgrows its space, snip it back with a pair of pruners.

Take cuttings in fall for a supply of new plants the next spring. Once they have rooted, keep the young plants in a cool, bright room over winter.

Tips

Licorice plant is a perennial grown as an annual. It is prized for its foliage rather than its flowers. Include it in your hanging baskets and container plantings to provide a soft, silvery backdrop for the colourful flowers of other plants. Licorice plant can also be used as a groundcover or as an edge in beds and borders. It will cascade down in rock gardens and along the tops of retaining walls.

This is a good indicator plant for hanging baskets. When you see licorice plant wilting, it is time to water your baskets.

Recommended

H. petiolare is a trailing plant with fuzzy grey-green leaves. Cultivars are more common than the species. The **Licorice Series** is especially popular and offers a varied group of interesting foliar plants, including 'Lemon Licorice' with velvety soft, pale lime foliage; 'Licorice Splash,' a bushier, compact cultivar with evenly variegated, pale green and white foliage; 'Petite Licorice' with fine foliage in a compact form and

H. petiolare 'Silver' (above)
H. petiolare 'Petite Licorice'

silvery green leaves; and finally 'White Licorice' with abundant, elegant, silver-frosted foliage. **'Limelight'** has bright, lime green leaves that need protection from direct sun to maintain their colour. **'Silver'** is a common cultivar with grey-green leaves covered in a silvery down. **'Silver Spike'** and **'Spike'** are newer, upright cultivars. A less common cultivar, **'Variegatum,'** has grey-green leaves dappled or margined in silvery cream.

Problems & Pests

Powdery mildew can be an occasional problem.

Lobelia
Edging Lobelia
Lobelia

Height: 10–25 cm (4–10")-**Spread:** equal to height-**Flower colour:** purple, blue, pink, white, red; attractive foliage

FOR QUITE SOME TIME, IT WAS DIFFICULT TO FIND A MIXED container with no lobelia planted in it. Although it will likely never lose its place in Alberta gardeners' hearts, lobelia's popularity has waned slightly because of the introduction of new bedding plants that provide a similar appeal. It was also often grown in inappropriate locations, resulting in a plant that would fade, thin and appear spent by mid-summer, to most gardeners' chagrin. To prevent this from happening, grow this pretty, colourful, little plant in a location that is protected from direct afternoon sun. With this sage advice in mind, you'll likely find yourself considering the fine qualities of lobelia from one spring to another.

Planting

Seeding: Indoors in mid-winter

Planting out: After last frost

Spacing: 15 cm (6")

Growing

Lobelia is often listed as a full sun annual, but it does better sited in **partial** or **light shade**. The soil should be **fertile, high in organic matter, moist** and **fairly well drained**. Lobelia likes cool summer nights. In hot weather, take care that its soil stays moist.

Lobelia seedlings are prone to damping off. See the section 'Starting Annuals from Seed' in the introduction for information on proper propagation techniques to help prevent this problem.

Tips

Use lobelia along the edges of beds and borders, on rock walls, in rock gardens, in mixed containers or in hanging baskets.

Trim lobelia back after the first wave of flowers. It will stop blooming in the hottest part of summer but will revive in fall if you continue to water it regularly over the summer.

Recommended

L. erinus may be rounded and bushy or low and trailing. It bears flowers in shades of blue, purple, red, pink or white. **Cascade Series** plants have a trailing form; flowers come in many shades. **'Crystal Palace'** is a compact plant that rarely grows over 10 cm (4") in height. This cultivar has dark green foliage and dark blue flowers. The cultivars in the **Regatta**

Cascade Series (above), 'Sapphire' (below)

Series are trailing; they tolerate heat better and bloom longer than other cultivars. **Riviera Series** are bushy plants with flowers in shades of blue and purple. **'Sapphire'** has white-centred blue flowers on trailing plants.

Problems & Pests

Rust, leaf spot and slugs may be troublesome.

Lotus Vine

Lotus

Height: 15–20 cm (6–8") **Spread:** 90 cm (36") or more
Flower colour: orange, red, yellow; attractive foliage

LOTUS VINE IS VALUED MORE FOR ITS FOLIAGE THAN ITS FLOWERS, adding a tropical flare to decorative containers regardless of style, colour or size. When allowed to drape over the edge of the container, lotus vine brings a softness to even the most brash and bold designs with its greyish green, soft, almost ferny foliage. This unusual trailing vine is a member of the legume family and bears fiery, exotic flowers. The flowers often don't appear in great numbers, however, because of our shorter season. Their bright colours add another unique element to the plant's overall appeal, drawing you in to see if they are real.

Planting

Seeding: Not recommended

Planting out: Spring, once soil has warmed and risk of frost has passed

Spacing: 15–30 cm (6–12")

Growing

Lotus vine prefers **full to partial sun**. The soil should be **moderately fertile** and **well drained**. This annual can tolerate hot and dry locations. Pinch the new tips back in late spring to early summer to promote bushier growth.

Tips

Lotus vine is often grown in containers of all shapes and sizes. Its cascading habit and striking, unique foliage are most effective when allowed to trail over the side of a decorative pot, window box or built-in planter. The flowers are bright and colourful in contrast to the silvery-green, ferny foliage and are complementary to purple and yellow flowering and foliar plants.

Recommended

L. x **'Amazon Sunset'** bears greyish green, needle-like foliage and vibrantly hued yellow-orange flowers that darken toward the edge.

L. berthelotii is a trailing plant with silvery stems covered in fine, soft, needle-like foliage from base to tip. Small clusters of vivid orange to scarlet flowers that resemble lobster claws emerge through the silvery leaves in spring and summer.

L. maculatus is another trailing species that closely resembles *L. berthelotii* in foliage and flowers. It also grows to a similar size.

L. berthelotii (photos this page)

Cultivars and hybrids are available for both species in various shades of yellow, orange, scarlet and red. However, it is difficult in most cases to reliably connect all cultivars and hybrids to one particular species.

L. x **'New Gold Flash'** is another hybrid that bears stunning orange and red striped blooms amid silvery stems and foliage.

Problems & Pests

Aphids and root rot can occur, but infrequently.

Love-in-a-Mist
Devil-in-a-Bush
Nigella

Height: 40–60 cm (16–24") **Spread:** 20–30 cm (8–12") **Flower colour:** blue, white, pink, purple; attractive foliage

THE COMMON NAME "LOVE-IN-A-MIST" REFERS TO THE FINE, hair-like bracts that encircle the flower, making it appear as though the flower blooms are floating in a greenish mist. This plant is also known as devil-in-a-bush because of the papery twisted seed pods that resemble the horns of the devil. Love-in-a-mist is perfectly suited to our climate and is a good choice for gardeners of every level. It is certainly unique, putting forth scads of flowers that few gardeners could ever be disappointed with. Deadhead to keep new flowers coming, or allow the plant to self-sow if you would like new plants to grow next spring.

Planting

Seeding: Indoors in late winter; direct sow in early spring

Planting out: Mid-spring

Spacing: 25–38 cm (10–15")

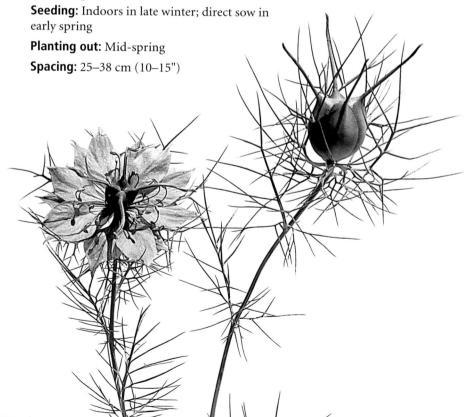

Growing

Love-in-a-mist prefers **full sun**. The soil should be of **average fertility, light** and **well drained**.

Direct sow seeds at two-week intervals throughout spring to prolong the blooming period. This plant resents having its roots disturbed. Seeds started indoors should be planted in peat pots or pellets to avoid damaging the roots when the plant is transplanted into the garden.

Love-in-a-mist has a tendency to self-sow and may show up in unexpected spots in your garden for years to come. Its ferny foliage and delicate blue flowers blend with most plants.

Tips

This attractive, airy plant is often used in mixed beds and borders. The flowers appear to float above the delicate foliage. The blooming may slow and the plants may die back if the weather gets too hot in summer.

The stems of this plant can be a bit floppy and may benefit from being staked with twiggy branches. Poke the branches in around the plants while they are young, and the plants will grow up between the twigs.

Recommended

N. damascena forms a loose mound of finely divided foliage. It grows 45–60 cm (18–24") tall and spreads about half this much. The light blue flowers darken as they mature. Plants in the **Miss Jekyll Series** grow to about 45 cm (18") high and

N. damascena (photos this page)

bear semi-double flowers in rose pink, sky blue or a deep cornflower blue that pairs especially well with golden yellow coreopsis. **'Mulberry Rose'** bears light pink flowers that mature to dark pink. **Persian Jewel Series** contains some of the most common cultivars, with plants that usually grow to 40 cm (16") tall and have flowers in many colours.

Madagascar Periwinkle

Catharanthus

Height: 30–60 cm (12–24") **Spread:** usually equal to or greater than height **Flower colour:** red, rose, pink, mauve, apricot, white, often with contrasting centres

NATIVE TO THE ISLAND OF MADAGASCAR, THIS FLOWERING ANNUAL is appreciated for its tolerance to dry conditions and poor soils. It is an undemanding plant that produces impatiens-like flowers all summer long. It thrives in the heat and works well in those reflective, hot areas in foundation plantings where other species fail. It's not uncommon to confuse this plant with either balsam or impatiens, but it is in a class all its own. Madagascar periwinkle was once classified as a member of the *Vinca* genus, but it has since been reclassified as *Catharanthus*, Greek for 'pure flower.'

Planting

Seeding: Indoors in mid-winter

Planting out: After last frost

Spacing: 20–45 cm (8–18")

Growing

Periwinkle prefers **full sun** but tolerates partial shade. Any **well-drained** soil is fine. This plant tolerates pollution and drought but prefers to be watered regularly. It doesn't like to be too wet, though, so take care not to overwater it. Avoid planting periwinkle in cold soil because it may fail to thrive. The soil temperature should be 12.5°–17.5° C (55°–64° F) for seeds to germinate.

Tips

Periwinkle will do well in the sunniest, warmest part of the garden. Plant it in a bed along an exposed driveway or against the south-facing wall of the house. It can also be used in hanging baskets, in planters and as a temporary groundcover.

This plant is a perennial that is grown as an annual. In a bright room, it can be grown as a houseplant.

Recommended

C. roseus (*Vinca rosea*) forms a mound of strong stems. The flowers are pink, red or white, often with contrasting centres. **'Apricot Delight'** bears pale apricot flowers with bright raspberry red centres. **Cooler Series** plants have light-coloured flowers with darker, contrasting centres. **'Pacifica'** is a compact plant with flowers in various colours.

C. roseus (photos this page)

Problems & Pests

Slugs can be troublesome. Most rot and other fungal problems can be prevented by not overwatering.

One of the best annuals to use in front of homes on busy streets, periwinkle will bloom happily despite exposure to exhaust fumes and dust.

Maidenhair Vine
Creeping Wirevine
Muehlenbeckia

Height: 10–15 cm (4–6") **Spread:** 45–60 cm (18–24")
Flower colour: inconspicuous flowers; grown for foliage

MAIDENHAIR VINE IS NEW TO THE MARKET AND HAS SLOWLY
worked its way onto the Alberta gardening scene. It is a tough little mounding vine, and in Alberta gardens, it lacks the invasive nature it displays in
much warmer climates with longer seasons. There are few other decorative
foliage "filler" plants for containers that also fit the trailing bill. Maidenhair
vine is also noted as being a deer-resistant plant, which is ideal for those in
rural areas. Its moderate growth, tiny, neat leaves and wiry stems make
maidenhair vine a great garden plant for those willing to attempt growing
plants into topiary forms too.

Planting

Seeding: Not recommended

Planting out: Spring, once ground has warmed and risk of frost has passed

Spacing: 10–20 cm (4–8")

Growing

Maidenhair vine grows well in locations with **full sun** with a **little mid-day shade. Moderately fertile, moist** but **well-drained** soil is best.

M. complexa (photos this page)

Tips

Maidenhair vine is ideal for containers where it can display its mounding and trailing habit. Its tiny leaves offset bolder-leaved plants and bright, vivid flowers, including coleus, osteospermum, petunias and marguerite daisies. Planting maidenhair vine in beds and borders is much less effective; it will get lost amid the other plants.

Recommended

M. complexa (maidenhair vine, wire vine, angel vine) is a vigorous, creeping or twining climber. It has slender, dark, wiry stems and tiny, rounded, green leaves. The species has a dense, mounding habit. The wiry stems eventually cascade over the edge of the container. **Var. microphylla** is identical in appearance and habit but produces leaves half the size of the species.

The common name wirevine was given because of the wiry stems that contort, curl and bend like fine floral wire.

Mexican Sunflower

Tithonia

Height: 60 cm–1.8 m (2–6') **Spread:** 30–60 cm (12–24")
Flower colour: orange, red-orange, yellow

KNOWING A PLANT'S NATIVE HABITAT IS HELPFUL WHEN TRYING
to determine what location and conditions it may prefer. The common
name, in this case, is a sure-fire give away. A native of Mexico and Central
America is bound to thrive in hot, sunny and dry conditions, and thrive it
does. One year my sister-in-law planted this on the hot, sunny side of her
garage. It thrived all right, bursting forth into a huge specimen that
impressed everyone. Its coarsely textured, dense foliage and fiery hot
flowers put on quite the show.

*For a hot look along
a sunny fence or wall,
mix Mexican sunflower
with other sunflowers
and marigolds.*

Planting

Seeding: Indoors in early spring; direct sow in spring

Planting out: Once soil has warmed

Spacing: 30–60 cm (12–24")

Growing

Mexican sunflower grows best in **full sun**. The soil should be of **average to poor fertility** and **well drained**. Cover seeds lightly because they germinate more evenly and quickly when exposed to some light. Mexican sunflower needs little water or care; however, it will bloom more profusely if it is deadheaded regularly.

Tips

Mexican sunflower is heat resistant, so it is ideal for growing in a sunny, dry, warm spot such as under the eaves of a south-facing wall. The plants are tall and break easily if exposed to too much wind; grow along a wall or fence to provide shelter and stability. This annual has a coarse appearance and is well suited to the back of a border, where it will provide a good backdrop to a bed of shorter plants.

Recommended

T. rotundifolia is a vigorous, bushy plant. It grows 90 cm–1.8 m (3–6') tall and spreads 30–60 cm (12–24"). Vibrant orange-red flowers are produced from mid- to late summer through to frost. The leaves and stems are covered in a downy fuzz. **'Fiesta del Sol'** bears bright orange flowers on plants that grow about 75 cm (30") tall. **'Goldfinger'** grows 60–90 cm (24–36") tall and bears

T. rotundifolia (above), *T. rotundifolia* 'Torch' (below)

large, orange flowers. **'Torch'** has bright red-orange flowers. **'Yellow Torch'** has bright yellow flowers.

Problems & Pests

This plant is generally resistant to most problems; however, young foliage may suffer slug and snail damage. Aphids can become a problem if not dealt with immediately.

Mignonette
Reseda

Height: 30–60 cm (12–24") **Spread:** 15–30 cm (6–12") **Flower colour:** yellow, reddish green; attractive foliage

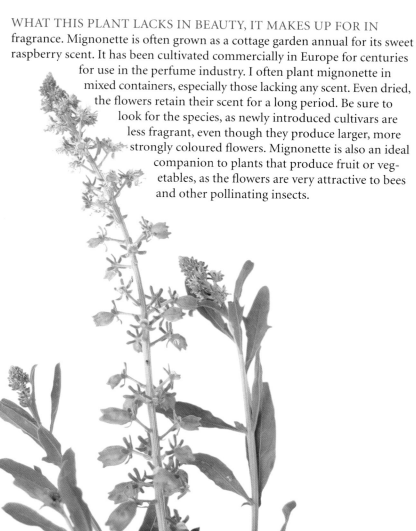

WHAT THIS PLANT LACKS IN BEAUTY, IT MAKES UP FOR IN fragrance. Mignonette is often grown as a cottage garden annual for its sweet raspberry scent. It has been cultivated commercially in Europe for centuries for use in the perfume industry. I often plant mignonette in mixed containers, especially those lacking any scent. Even dried, the flowers retain their scent for a long period. Be sure to look for the species, as newly introduced cultivars are less fragrant, even though they produce larger, more strongly coloured flowers. Mignonette is also an ideal companion to plants that produce fruit or vegetables, as the flowers are very attractive to bees and other pollinating insects.

Planting

Seeding: Start indoors in late winter or direct sow in mid-spring.

Planting out: Around last frost

Spacing: About 22.5 cm (9") apart

Growing

Mignonette grows well in **full sun** or **partial shade**. Soil should be of **average fertility, slightly alkaline** and **well drained**. Deadheading will prolong the flowering period.

Tips

Mignonette can be included in a mixed border, preferably near a window, patio or a frequently used path, so the scent can be enjoyed. Because of its subtle appearance, it also works well in a wild garden setting, meadow or naturalized area. Combine mignonette with showier plants for visual as well as olfactory stimulation.

R. odorata (photos this page)

Recommended

R. odorata is a bushy, upright plant. It grows 30–60 cm (12–24") tall and spreads 15–30 cm (6–12"). The plants are grown for the long-lasting fragrance of their inconspicuous reddish green flowers. Some newer cultivars have more decorative flowers but are not as scented. '**Fragrant Beauty**' has red-tinged, green flowers and a very sweet fragrance.

Mignonette attracts bees and other pollen-loving insects to the garden.

Million Bells
Calibrachoa, Trailing Petunia
Calibrachoa

Height: 15–30 cm (6–12") **Spread:** up to 60 cm (24") **Flower colour:** pink, purple, yellow, apricot, red-orange, white, blue; attractive foliage

AS THE NAME IMPLIES, YOU GET A LOT OF FLOWER BANG FOR YOUR buck with million bells. As relatives of the petunia, the flowers resemble petunia blossoms but in miniature. They also flower similarly to petunia, bearing hundreds of flowers continuously throughout the growing season. Million bells are still relatively new to the market but have become incredibly popular. Their wide array of colours, ranging from terracotta to magenta pink, complements their trailing habit as they spill over the edge of containers or hanging baskets. Some of the most well-known breeders worldwide have been adding annually to the cache of million bells, allowing gardeners to take full advantage of the colours and forms available on the market.

Planting

Seeding: Seeds may not be available

Planting out: After last frost

Spacing: 15–38 cm (6–15")

Growing

Million bells plants prefer **full sun** for peak flowering but can tolerate some shade. The soil should be **fertile, moist** and **well drained**. Though it prefers to be watered regularly, million bells is fairly drought resistant once established. It will bloom well into fall; the flowers become hardier over summer and as the weather cools.

Tips

Popular for planters and hanging baskets, million bells is also attractive in beds and borders. It grows all summer and needs plenty of room to spread or it will overtake other flowers. Pinch back to keep plants compact. In a hanging basket, it will produce plentiful, bell-shaped blooms.

To protect the petals from rain, place hanging baskets under the eaves of the house or porch.

Recommended

Calibrachoa **hybrids** have a dense, trailing habit. They bear small flowers that look like petunias. The **Million Bells Series** includes 'Cherry Pink,' with reddish pink flowers on upright plants as well as 'Terra Cotta,' bearing flowers made up of red, orange and yellow; and 'Yellow,' which has unusually clear, bright yellow flowers. The **Minifamous Series** offers vivid, strong colour selections with bright yellow

C. Million Bells Series 'Terra Cotta' (above); C. Million Bells Series 'Trailing Pink,' 'Trailing Blue' and 'Cherry Pink' (below)

throats. The **Superbells Series** of hybrids is more heat tolerant and includes a wide variety of colours to choose from. Blue, cherry red, coral pink, pink, pink kiss, red, trailing blue and rose and white are available in this series, both in compact and trailing forms.

Problems & Pests

Wet weather and cloudy days may cause leaf spot and delayed blooming. Slugs like to nibble on the petals.

Nemesia

Nemesia

Height: 15–60 cm (6–24") **Spread**: 10–30 cm (4–12") **Flower colour**: red, blue, purple, pink, white, yellow, orange or bicoloured; attractive foliage

ALMOST EVERY PHYSICAL ATTRIBUTE OF NEMESIA IS PERFECTLY suited to container culture. Available in a wide array of colour combinations, the flowers resemble tiny snapdragons, often bearing varied shades of yellow on their bottom lip, which gives them a pouting appearance. The Sunsatia hybrids, a German hybridizing breakthrough, is like nothing else on the market. This series exhibits colours from glowing canary yellows to buttery pastels. This group of hybrids holds its own in both cool and hot temperatures, and is outstanding in hanging baskets, borders and window boxes. The names alone are enough to draw you in, but you better have a full tummy. Selections like coconut, banana, pineapple, peach, lemon and cranberry are bound to leave you wanting more.

Planting

Seeding: Start indoors in early spring

Planting out: After last frost

Spacing: 15 cm (6")

Growing

Nemesias prefer **full sun**. The soil should be **average to fertile, slightly acidic, moist** and **well drained**. Regular watering will keep these plants blooming through the summer.

Tips

Nemesias make a bright and colourful addition to the front of a mixed border or mixed container planting.

Recommended

N. caerulea (*N. fruticans*) is a bushy plant that grows up to 60 cm (24") tall and spreads about 30 cm (12"). It bears blue, pink, purple or white flowers. Several cultivars are available as transplants. **'Blue Bird'** bears lavender blue flowers on plants 20–30 cm (8–12") tall. **'Blue Lagoon'** also grows 20–30 cm (8–12") tall producing slate blue flowers. **'Candy Girl'** bears frilled, fragrant, light pink flowers on 25–30 cm (10–12") tall plants. **'Compact Innocence'** grows 25–30-cm (10–12") tall, while **'Innocence'** grows 30–35 cm (12–14") tall. Both have fragrant, lilac-scented, white flowers. These varieties can all be planted out in early spring and will tolerate frost and cool temperatures but are also very heat tolerant when fertilized regularly. **Safari Series** plants are vigorous growers that reach 20–35 cm (8–14") tall and have good heat tolerance and fragrant flowers. **'Safari Pink'** has pink flowers. **'Safari Plum'** bears large, purple flowers.

N. strumosa forms a bushy mound of bright green foliage. It grows 15–30 cm (6–12") tall and spreads

N. strumosa 'KLM'

10–20 cm (4–8"). It bears flowers in shades of blue, purple, white, pink, red or yellow, often in bicolours. **Carnival Series** plants bear many flowers in yellow, white, orange, pink or red on compact plants. **'KLM'** has bicoloured blue and white flowers with yellow throats. **'National Ensign'** ('Red and White') bears flowers bicoloured red and white.

N. x Sunsatia Hybrids is a series of award-winning, versatile plants including **'Sunsatia Banana'** which bears flowers in a wonderful blend of yellows ranging from cream to medium yellow. **'Sunsatia Coconut'** is the most heat tolerant of the series, bearing lightly fragrant, white flowers with yellow throats. **'Sunsatia Cranberry'** has rich red flowers while **'Sunsatia Peach,'** a compact variety, has lightly fragrant, creamy, light yellow and violet bicoloured flowers, reminiscent of tiny violas.

Problems & Pests

Occasional problems with crown or root rot are possible.

Nemophila
Nemophila

Height: 15–30 cm (6–12") **Spread:** 30 cm (12") **Flower colour:** blue, white, purple; attractive foliage

NEMOPHILA HAS BEEN IN GARDENING CIRCLES FOR QUITE SOME time now but still falls under the radar. It is deserving of more use in the prairie landscape. Even with all of the new introductions on the market, nemophila can hold its own, offering an old-fashioned charm that still has a place in the garden. Two species are available with distinctly different flowers. Baby blue eyes, or *N. menziesii,* bears slightly larger flowers than its close relative in pale shades of blue atop ornate, ferny foliage. Five-spot, or *N. maculata,* is a fun species, bearing white flowers with purple veins and a purple spot at the tip of each petal. The cultivars provide colour combinations rarely found in flowers, allowing you to create the most amazing combinations possible.

These plants may cease flowering during the hottest part of summer if they are allowed to completely dry out.

Planting

Seeding: Direct sow around last frost

Planting out: If necessary, after last frost

Spacing: 20–30 cm (8–12")

Growing

Nemophila grows well in **full sun** or **partial shade**. The soil should be **fertile, moist** and **well drained**. Do not let the soil dry out completely. Shelter this plant from strong winds and avoid placing it near paths, where the tender foliage may be damaged by passersby.

This plant resents being transplanted and should be sown directly into the garden. It can be started indoors in peat pots or pellets in early spring if desired.

N. menziesii 'Penny Black' (photos this page)

Tips

Use nemophila as an annual groundcover or as edging for borders. It works well in mixed planters, hanging baskets and window boxes.

Recommended

N. maculata (five-spot) is a low, mound-forming plant. It grows up to 30 cm (12") tall, with an equal spread. The white flowers have purple veins, and each of the five petals has a single purple spot at the tip, giving the plant its common name.

N. menziesii (baby blue-eyes) is a low, spreading plant 15–25 cm (6–10") tall and 30 cm (12") wide. The flowers are blue with white centres. **Subsp.** *atomaria* ('Snowstorm') has slightly off-white flowers spotted purple-black. **'Pennie Black'** has very dark purple flowers with silvery white edges.

Problems & Pests

Aphids and powdery mildew can cause problems.

Ornamental Cabbage
Ornamental Kale
Brassica

Height: 30–60 cm (12–24") **Spread:** 30–60 cm (12–24")
Flower colour: grown for foliage

I ONCE SAW A BEAUTIFUL FRESH FLORAL ARRANGEMENT FILLED with Sunrise and Sunset stems, and I was instantly hooked. Shortly after, I saw a fall flowerbed filled with some of the larger ornamental cabbage selections. The large, frilly, ruffled heads of tightly packed leaves were showing off their bright shades of purple, pink, and cream. Ornamental cabbage is often planted for late-season interest, as it really begins to show off when most other plants, both perennials and annuals, are looking spent. As the autumn days and nights grow cooler, ornamental cabbage's colours intensify and deepen. It is best planted with other colourful plants, otherwise it can resemble an abandoned veggie patch. Plant staggered rows of cabbage with coleus, pansies and snapdragons to complement their cool tones.

Planting

Seeding: Direct sow in spring

Transplanting: Spring to late summer; from six-packs

Spacing: 45–60 cm (18–24")

Growing

Ornamental cabbage prefers to grow in **full sun** but tolerates partial shade. The soil should be **fertile, well drained** and **moist**. Ornamental cabbage also prefers soil with a **neutral to slightly alkaline pH.**

Ornamental cabbage plants can be started in seedbeds or trays and transplanted in spring. Many packages of seeds contain a variety of cultivars.

The plant colours brighten after a light frost or when the air temperature drops below 10° C (50° F).

Tips

Ornamental cabbage is a tough, bold plant that is at home in the vegetable garden as well as in the border of flowerbeds.

Wait until some true leaves develop before thinning. When thinning seedlings, use those that are not transplanted in a salad.

Recommended

B. oleracea (Acephala group) forms loose, erect rosettes of large, often fringed leaves in shades of purple, red, pink and white. It grows 30–60 cm (12–24") tall with an equal spread. Plants of this species are biennials, producing flowers in shades of white to yellow in the second year. The **Kamome Series** is a ruffled leaf form with red and white foliage. **Northern Lights Series** produce

B. oleracea cultivar

45–60 cm (18–24") wide heads of frilled foliage in shades of grey green, creamy white, pale and dark purple. **'Osaka,'** from the **Dynasty Series,** grows 30 cm (12") tall and wide with wavy foliage that is red to pink in the centre and blue-green to the outside. **'Sunrise'** and **'Sunset'** are new small-headed, long-stemmed plants used as long-lasting cut flowers, in creamy white, pink and red coloured foliage. They grow up to 60 cm (24") tall.

Problems & Pests

Ornamental cabbage is affected by a large range of pests and diseases including caterpillars, leaf miners, aphids, root maggots, cabbage worm (white butterfly), nematodes, plant bugs, flea beetles, leaf spot, clubroot and damping off.

Ornamental cabbage may also suffer nutrient deficiency problems.

Osteospermum

Osteospermum

Height: 30–50 cm (12–20") **Spread:** 25–50 cm (10–20") **Flower colours:** white, peach, orange, yellow, pink, lavender, purple, red; often with dark centres of blue-purple or other colours.

OSTEOSPERMUMS AREN'T EXACTLY NEW, BUT IN POPULARITY, they are gaining on the likes of petunias and pansies. They offer brightly coloured flowers in a unique selection of shades, with dark violet blue centres. These daisy-like flowers are unfazed by early spring frosts and excessive summer heat. When mass planted in large window boxes, they can give your house a storybook-like charm. Osteospermums are like the new daisy of the millennium, exhibiting vividly hued petals and outstanding performance. All they require, other than a little love and lots of sunshine, is a quick shearing in late summer and regular fertilizing to feed their big appetites.

Planting

Seeding: Indoors in early spring

Planting out: Late spring; if hardened off, they can withstand light frosts

Spacing: 30–45 cm (12–18")

Growing

Plant in **full sun** in **light, evenly moist, moderately fertile, well-drained** soil. Do not overwater or let the plants wilt. Weekly feeding with a well-balanced, water-soluble fertilizer that is high in nitrogen will keep them flowering all summer long. Use an organic mulch to cut down on the plants' water needs. Deadhead to encourage new growth and more flowers. Young plants can be pinched to encourage bushiness.

Tips

Osteospermum are tender perennials and subshrubs from South Africa that we use as annuals. Recent breeding work has made

O. *ecklonis* cultivar (above)
O. Symphony Series (below)

osteospermum much more likely to thrive in prairie gardens. They are best used in containers or beds, and their daisy flowers are great mixed with other plants like petunias or verbena.

Recommended

O. ecklonis is a variable subshrub that can grow upright to almost prostrate. The species is almost never grown in favour of its wonderful cultivars. **Passion Mix** are

free-flowering, heat-tolerant plants growing 30 cm (12") tall and 25 cm (10") wide. The flowers come in pink, rose, purple and pure white and have deep blue centres. This series was an All-America Selections winner in 1999. **Springstar Series** are compact, early flowering plants. 'Arctur' grows 36–40 cm (14–16") tall and wide and produces white flowers. 'Aurora' grows 25–33 cm (10–13") tall and wide and bears magenta to lavender flowers. 'Capella' is heat tolerant, growing 36–40 cm (14–16") tall and wide. It produces large white flowers. 'Mira' grows 36–40 cm (14–16") tall and wide, producing purple to deep magenta flowers with good heat tolerance. 'Sirius' bears magenta to-deep red flowers with elongated petals. It grows 45–50 cm (18–20") tall and wide. **Starwhirls Series** grow 30–45 cm (12–18") tall and wide. They have unique, spoon-shaped petals.

O. Symphony Series 'Lemon' (above)
O. ecklonis Starwhirls Series (below)

'**Starwhirls Antaris**' bears deep pink flowers. The petals of '**Starwhirls Vega**' are white on the upper surface and musky pink beneath.

O. Symphony Series from Proven Winners are mounding plants growing 25–38 cm (10–15") tall and wide. '**Cream**' has cream flowers. '**Lemon**' has lemon yellow flowers. '**Orange**' grows slightly smaller and has wonderful tangerine orange flowers. '**Peach**' bears lightly flushed peach/pink flowers. '**Vanilla**' bears white flowers. The Symphony Series is very heat tolerant and flowers well through the summer.

Problem & Pests

Problems with downy mildew, *Verticillium* wilt and aphids may occur. Fungal diseases can form if summer temperatures are high and rainy/overwatering conditions exist.

O. ecklonis cultivar (above)
O. Symphony Series 'Cream' and 'Orange' (below)

You may find the genus for this group of plants listed as either Dimorphotheca *or* Osteospermum. Dimorphotheca *is a closely related genus that formerly included all the plants now listed as* Osteospermum.

Oxalis

Oxalis

Height: 12.5–30 cm (5–12") **Spread:** 17.5–30 cm (7–12") or more **Flower colour:** yellow, white, pink, red; also grown for foliage

AFTER SEEING A PICTURE OF O. 'SAFFRON' PLANTED IN A VINTAGE, wall-mounted mailbox, peaking out of the little door, I had to find this plant. Oxalis' clover-like appearance immediately makes most people think of the weedy, albeit cute, clover that grows vigorously in our lawns, but this species is different. Over the last five or so years, it has been grown and bred by some of the leading breeders, including Proven Winners. I wouldn't recommend planting this group of plants in flowerbeds but highly recommend it for containers of all shapes and sizes. It readily fills those little spaces with dense, lustrous foliage and teeny, tiny flowers that never cease to amaze.

Planting

Seeding: Indoors in late winter or early spring

Planting out: Spring, once soil has warmed and risk of frost has passed

Spacing: 12.5–25 cm (5–10")

Growing

Oxalis prefers **full** or **partial sun** for optimum flowering but tolerates full shade. **Moderately fertile, humus-rich, well-drained** soil is best.

Tips

Oxalis is becoming increasingly popular in container culture, with new varieties appearing annually. Its tightly packed, fine foliage and prolific flowering are qualities ideal for containers of all sizes and styles. Oxalis works well mixed with other plants and is equally as stunning when planted alone to fill an entire hanging basket. For those fearful gardeners who are suspect of the invasive qualities of oxalis, try planting one or two in a retaining wall or trough garden.

The recommended species are not hardy to the prairies and will die off with a hard frost in the fall.

Recommended

O. crassipes is a vigorous species with bright green leaves and lemon yellow flowers. However, the cultivars are often available over the species. **'Alba'** (GARDEN HARDY WHITE) is a mound-forming cultivar with green leaves and tiny, white flowers. It is tolerant to extreme heat and drought. **'Rosea'** (GARDEN HARDY PINK) has pink flowers.

O. hedysaroides is more of an upright species that produces light green foliage and funnel-shaped, yellow flowers. It can grow up to 90 cm (36") tall and 45 cm (18") wide. **'Rubrum'** has red leaves and bright yellow flowers.

O. hedysaroides 'Rubrum' (above)

O. herrerae (*O. succulenta*) produces clusters of mid-green leaves on shorter stems than other species. Bowl-shaped, red-veined yellow flowers are produced in mid-summer. The species grows 30 cm (12") tall and 20 cm (8") wide. **'Saffron'** produces bold blue-green foliage and large, yellow flowers.

O. vulcanicola is a small, bushy spreading plant with reddish stems, green foliage flushed with red and yellow flowers with purple-red veining. It grows 20–70 cm (8–27½") tall with an equal or greater spread. **'Copper Tones'** has gold foliage with a touch of rust and buttery yellow flowers at the tip of reddish stems. **'Zinfandel'** produces dark burgundy, almost black foliage and tiny, vivid yellow blooms.

Problems & Pests

Rust and powdery mildew are remote possibilities.

Painted-Tongue
Velvet Flower
Salpiglossis

Height: up to 60 cm (24") **Spread:** 30 cm (12") **Flower colour:** blue, red, yellow, orange, pink, purple; often patterned bicolours

PAINTED-TONGUE WAS A FAVOURITE OF THE VICTORIANS, WHO loved its rich, jewel tones of gold, red, pink and blue. These plants can either be willowy or bushy, depending on the variety you choose. Painted-tongue blooms from mid-summer until frost, without hesitation. It looks best when grouped with plants that bear white flowers; the simplicity of the white blooms will offset painted-tongue's vivid flowers, showing off their exquisite markings. Birders are fond of this plant because the flowers are known to attract hummingbirds. Florists love it, too, for its long-lasting adornment of vases and floral arrangements. And gardeners thought they were the only ones who adored this plant!

The iridescent quality of these flowers causes their colour to change as they move in a breeze.

Planting

Seeding: Indoors in late winter; direct sow in spring

Planting out: After last frost

Spacing: 30 cm (12")

Growing

Painted-tongue prefers **full sun** but tolerates light shade. The soil should be **fertile, rich in organic matter** and **well drained**. A location sheltered from heavy rain and wind will keep these plants looking their best.

As with many members of the potato/tomato family, the seeds of painted-tongue are very tiny and shouldn't be covered with soil. They will germinate more evenly if kept in darkness until they sprout—place pots in a dark closet or cover them with dark plastic or layers of newspaper. Once they start to sprout, the plants can be moved to a well-lit location.

Tips

Painted-tongue is useful in the middle or back of beds and borders. It can also be added to large, mixed containers. Most types of painted-tongue can become battered in rain and wind, so plant this flower in a warm, sheltered area of the garden.

Recommended

S. sinuata is an upright species in the same family as petunias. '**Blue Peacock**' has blue flowers with yellow throats and dark veins. Plants of the **Casino Series**, with flowers in a wide range of colours, bloom early and tolerate rain and wind. **Royale Series** has flowers with more pronounced veining in the throat.

S. sinuata (photos this page)

Problems & Pests

Occasional problems with aphids or root rot are possible.

Pansy
Viola

Height: 7.5–25 cm (3–10") **Spread:** 15–30 cm (6–12") **Flower colour:** blue, purple, red, orange, yellow, pink, white, multi-coloured; attractive foliage

WHAT PERSON HAS NOT SEEN A PANSY AND MENTIONED ITS CUTE little "face"? What child hasn't planted these little beauties, lovingly cut them and taken them to his or her mother? We're all familiar with this tough little annual, but it's interesting to note that the common name pansy comes from the French word *pensee*, meaning "remembrance" or "thought," perhaps relating to a time when a bouquet of pansies was given to someone to express the sentiment, "I'm thinking of you." The pansy has drawn us in with its charm and delicate perfume for centuries. It also has an interesting history linked forever to the viola, its equally hardy but delicate ancestor. Violas were familiar to people living in Greece as far back as 4th century BC, and cultivated by them for herbal and medicinal use.

Planting

Seeding: Indoors in early winter or mid-summer

Planting out: Early spring or early fall

Spacing: 15 cm (6")

Growing

Pansies prefer **full sun** but tolerate partial shade. The soil should be **fertile, moist** and **well drained**.

V. x *wittrockiana* (photos this page)

Pansies do best when the weather is cool. They may die back completely in summer. Plants may rejuvenate in fall, but it is often easier to plant new ones in fall and not take up summer garden space with plants that don't look their best.

Direct sowing is not recommended. Sow seeds indoors in early winter for spring flowers and in mid-summer for fall and early-winter blooms. More seeds will germinate if they are kept in darkness until they sprout. Place seed trays in a dark closet or cover with dark plastic or layers of newspaper to block out the light.

Tips

Pansies can be used in beds and borders, and they are popular for mixing in with spring-flowering bulbs. They can also be grown in containers. The large-flowered pansies are preferred for early-spring colour among primroses in garden beds.

Recommended

V. cornuta (horned violet, viola) is low-growing, about 15 cm (6") tall and 30–40 cm (12–16") wide. The flowers are smaller than pansies and larger than Johnny-jump-ups, usually in shades of blue, purple or white with the distinctive and charming "face" pattern violas are known for. **'Bambini'** produces flowers in a wider range of colours including shades of pink, yellow, orange, blue, purple and white. **Chalon Hybrids** bear a rich mix of blue, red, rose and

white bicoloured and multicoloured flowers. Each colourful petal is ruffled. **Sorbet Series** is popular for the plants' wide colour range and cold tolerance. Planted in fall, they flower until the ground freezes and may surprise you with another show in spring. **'Sorbet Yesterday, Today and Tomorrow'** bears flowers that open white and gradually turn purple as they mature.

V. tricolor (Johnny-jump-up) is a popular species. The flowers are purple, white and yellow, usually in combination, although several varieties have flowers in a single colour, often purple. This plant thrives in gravel. **'Bowles Black'** has dark purple flowers that appear almost black. The centre of each flower is yellow. **'Helen Mound'** ('Helen Mount') bears large flowers in the traditional purple, yellow and white combination.

V.* x *wittrockiana (pansy) comes in blue, purple, red, orange, yellow, pink and white, often multicoloured or with face-like markings.

V. x *wittrockiana* (photos this page)

Antique Shades Mix offers pastel combinations of plum, yellow, apricot, rust and cream. **Can Can Mix** bears frilly flowers with ruffled edges, in bicolour and multicolour combinations of yellow, purple, red, white, pink and blue. **'Floral Dance'** is popular for spring and fall displays as it is quite cold hardy; it has flowers in a variety of solid colours and multi-colours. **Imperial Series** includes plants that bear large flowers in a range of unique colours. 'Imperial Frosty Rose' has flowers with deep rose pink centres that gradually pale to white near the edges of the petals. **Joker Series** has bicoloured or multi-coloured flowers with distinctive face markings. The flowers come in all colours. **'Maxim Marina'** bears light blue flowers with white-rimmed, dark blue blotches at the centre. This cultivar tolerates both hot and cold temperatures. **Watercolour Series** is a newer group of cultivars with flowers in delicate pastel shades.

V. tricolor (above), *V.* x *wittrockiana* (below)

Problems & Pests

Slugs and snails can be problems. Fungal problems can be avoided through good air circulation and good drainage.

Passion Flower

Passiflora

Height: up to 9 m (30') **Spread:** variable **Flower colour:** white or pale pink petals with blue or purple bands; attractive foliage

PASSION FLOWER IS A PLANT THAT CAN BE ENJOYED YEAR-ROUND. Placing it outdoors in a sunny spot during the summer months is guaranteed to promote lush, new foliage and a wealth of flowers, at least until the meteorologists start forecasting cold temperatures on autumn nights. This is when it's time to bring the plant inside for winter. It should be quarantined for a short while to ensure that you haven't brought any critters inside. Cut it back by at least one-third and give it a gentle, tepid bath to wash the grime and bugs away. You'll be surprised to know that it will likely even bloom indoors in the right location, and it will remain a lush, green houseplant until the following spring.

Planting

Seeding: Not recommended

Planting out: Several weeks after the last frost

Spacing: 30 cm (12")

Growing

Grow passion flower in **full sun** or **partial shade**. This plant prefers **well-drained, moist soil** of **average fertility**. Keep it sheltered from wind and cold.

Germination is erratic and propagation is generally easier from cuttings, but for gardeners who like a challenge, it is possible to propagate passion flower from seed. Soak seeds for 24 hours in hot water before planting. Place the seed tray in full sun because the seeds need light to germinate. Keep the soil moist and at about 15° C (59° F).

Tips

Passion flower is a popular addition to mixed containers and makes an unusual focal point near a door or other entryway. This plant is actually a fast-growing, woody climber that is grown as an annual.

Many garden centres now sell small passion flower plants in spring. They quickly climb trellises and other supports over summer. They can be composted at the end of summer or cut back and brought inside to enjoy in a bright room over winter.

The small round fruits are edible but not very tasty.

P. caerulea

Recommended

P. caerulea (blue passion flower) bears unusual purple-banded, purple-white flowers all summer. **'Constance Elliott'** bears fragrant white flowers.

Problems & Pests

Spider mites, whiteflies, scale insects and nematodes may cause occasional trouble.

The common name is said to refer to Christ's passion. The three stigmas of the flower are said to represent the nails and the five anthers the wounds.

Pentas

Pentas

Height: 60–90 cm (24–36") **Spread:** 60–90 cm (24–36") **Flower colour:** pink, red, purple, magenta, white

ALL PENTAS SELECTIONS ARE EXTREMELY ATTRACTIVE TO butterflies, and the red and dark pink varieties delight hummingbirds. The large clusters of flowers are offset by equally large leaves and create a nice backdrop to smaller plants. They are a great substitute in size and height for a few of the more traditional annuals, including geraniums and upright petunias. Pentas also make a colourful splash in the tropical-themed gardens that have become the recent trend. The flower stems are useful for fresh arrangements so they can be enjoyed equally indoors. It's not hard to understand why prairie dwellers rarely take tropical themes and vivid flower colours for granted. It is the prairies after all.

Planting

Seeding: Indoors in late winter or direct sow in spring

Transplanting: Late spring

Spacing: 60 cm (24")

Growing

Pentas grows best in **full sun** and **well-drained, moist, fertile** soil. Ensure you provide adequate water. Propagate pentas plants from seed or softwood cuttings in summer. Regular deadheading will encourage more blooms.

P. lanceolata (photos this page)

Tips

Use pentas in a bed or border where the coarse foliage will provide a backdrop for smaller plants at the front. Pentas also does very well as an outdoor container plant and is often sold during winter as a house-plant. Cuttings taken from these houseplants can be grown outside the following summer.

Pinch back the tips for a more compact, bushier plant.

Recommended

P. lanceolata is a subshrub grown as an annual. It has an erect, sometimes-prostrate, growth habit and produces flat-topped clusters of star-shaped, pink, red, purple or white flowers in summer. The **Butterfly Series** has light pink to white, cherry red and hot cherry red with a white eye, deep pink, light lavender and bright red flowers. **Graffiti Mix** is a brand new introduction, offering compact plants with pink, red, rose, violet and white flowers. **New Look Series** offers solid-coloured selections of white, red, rose, pink

and violet. **'Stars and Stripes'** has green and white variegated leaves with red flowers.

Problems & Pests

Aphids and spider mites may cause problems. Check the plants carefully when purchasing.

Persian Shield

Strobilanthes

Height: 45–90 cm (18–36") **Spread:** 60–90 cm (24–36") **Flower colour:** blue; plant grown for green, purple and silver foliage

PERSIAN SHIELD IS GROWN STRICTLY FOR ITS FOLIAGE; THE LITTLE flowers are just an afterthought with this showy foliage plant. It is most effective in locations and with plants that play off of the colourful, almost-garish colouration of the leaves. Partially shaded borders are a fine location, where its unique silvery purple sheen outdoes most flowers. It is an excellent plant for containers and a real attention grabber when planted with plants producing lime-green, grey, silver or variegated foliage. Gardeners are very fond of this plant, but deer and rabbits don't like it at all, so the neighbour-hood wildlife won't be nibbling it. Persian shield can also take the heat and makes a wonderful houseplant throughout the winter, right alongside your passion flower.

Planting

Seeding: Not recommended

Planting out: After last frost, in warm soil

Spacing: 60 cm (24")

Growing

Persian shield grows well in **full sun** and **partial shade**. The soil should be **average to fertile, light** and **very well drained**. Pinch growing tips to encourage bushiness or the plant will tend to be lanky.

Tips

The colourful foliage provides a dramatic background in annual or mixed borders and in container plantings. Combine with yellow- or white-flowered plants for a stunning contrast.

Root cuttings or tip cuttings can be started in late summer if you'd like indoor plants for winter.

Recommended

S. dyerianus is a tender shrub that is grown as an annual. It forms a bushy mound of silver- or purple-flushed foliage with contrasting dark green or purple veins and margins. The foliage emerges purple and matures to silver. Plants may produce spikes of blue flowers in early fall.

Problems & Pests

Trouble with root rot is possible in very wet soils.

This tropical shrub from Burma adds a cool, shimmery touch to the front of a sunny bed or to a large, container planting.

S. dyerianus (photos this page)

Petunia

Petunia

Height: 15–45 cm (6–18") **Spread:** 30–60 cm (12–24") or more
Flower colour: pink, purple, red, white, yellow, coral, blue or bicoloured

HAVE YOU FELT A LITTLE OVERWHELMED WITH THE EVER-GROWING selection of petunias? I suppose it's easy to feel like they're beginning to take over with their amazing variety of colours and combinations of frilly petals, veined petals, creepers, uprights and so on. They are even available in three different flower sizes! No self-respecting gardener would deny that there is a petunia for every gardening purpose. This member of the *Solanaceae* family, a relative of the potato, contains various substances that are poisonous to many insects, so it serves as a repellant, helping to keep pests away from other plants. You're looking at petunias in a whole new light, aren't you?

The name petunia is derived from petun, *the Brazilian word for tobacco, which comes from species of the related genus* Nicotiana.

Planting

Seeding: Indoors in mid-winter

Planting out: After last frost

Spacing: 30–45 cm (12–18")

Growing

Petunias prefer **full sun**. The soil should be of **average to rich fertility, light, sandy** and **well drained**. When sowing, press seeds into the soil surface but don't cover them with soil. Pinch halfway back in mid-summer to keep plants bushy and to encourage new growth and flowers.

Tips

Use petunias in beds, borders, containers and hanging baskets.

Recommended

P. x *hybrida* is a large group of popular, sun-loving annuals that fall into three categories: grandifloras, multifloras and millifloras.

The **grandiflora** petunias have the largest flowers—up to 10 cm (4") across. They have the widest variety of colours and forms, but they are the most likely to be damaged by heavy rain. **Daddy Series** plants are available in darkly veined shades of pink and purple. The **Frillytunia Series** is available in pink, burgundy and white. Each flower has a ruffled, frilly edge. **'Prism Sunshine'** is a 1998 All-America Selections winner. Its compact plants bear pale yellow flowers with deeper yellow throats. **Supercascade Series** come in a wide variety of colours. Cultivars in the **Ultra Series** are available in many colours, including bicolours, and

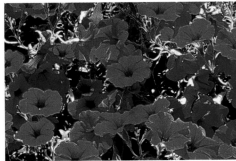

P. multiflora type 'Purple Wave' (above)
P. milliflora type 'Fantasy' (centre)

P. milliflora type (below)

'Tidal Wave Silver' (above)

Grandiflora type (centre), 'Blue Wave' (below)

recover quite quickly from weather damage.

Compared to the grandifloras, the **multiflora** petunias have smaller blooms (about half the size), bear many more flowers and tolerate adverse weather conditions better. **Carpet Series** plants are available in a wide variety of colours. **'Priscilla'** is an attractive mounding plant with pale mauve flowers with darker purple veining. Most of the flowers have a second ring of smaller ruffled petals in the centre of the flower. **Surfinia Series** plants branch freely, are self-cleaning and form a neat mound covered by a mass of flowers in shades of pink, blue, purple and white. Look for new additions to the series, which feature double flowers, minis, pastel colours and decorative veining. **Wave Series** plants are available in pink, purple and coral. Their low, spreading habit makes these plants popular as ground-covers and for hanging baskets and containers. The plants recover well

from rain damage, bloom nonstop, tolerate cold and spread quickly.

The **milliflora** petunias are the newest group. The flowers are about 2.5 cm (1") across and are borne profusely over the whole plant. These plants tolerate wet weather very well and sometimes self-seed. They are popular in mixed containers and hanging baskets and are also very nice in garden beds, forming neat mounds of foliage and flowers. **Fantasy Series** has plants in shades of red, purple, pink and white, although the pinks tend to be easiest to find. With the growing popularity of the millifloras, more colours will likely become available.

Problems & Pests

Aphids and fungi may present problems. Fungal problems can be avoided by wetting the foliage as little as possible and by providing a location with good drainage.

'Merlin Blue Morn' (above)

'Purple Wave' (centre), 'Lavender Wave' (below)

Pimpernel
Anagallis

Height: 15–45 cm (6–18") **Spread:** 20–45 cm (8–18") **Flower colour:** red, white, blue, pink, orange

PIMPERNEL HAS LONG BEEN REGARDED AS A RELIABLE ORNAMENTAL plant for the garden but was also used as a medicinal herb long ago. It was once highly regarded in the treatment of epilepsy, among other conditions, but was later deemed toxic. A homeopathic, topical remedy made from this plant is still used today for the removal of warts, but walking through the pimpernel won't take care of this problem alone. Similar to other annuals, the flowers are known to open early in the morning and close by mid-afternoon. Overcast conditions will also cause the flowers to close, and these plants are said to foretell inclement weather if they close earlier than expected.

Pimpernels are in the same family as primroses.

Planting

Seeding: Start indoors in late winter

Planting out: Around last frost

Spacing: 30–45 cm (12–18")

Growing

Pimpernels prefer **full sun**. The soil should be **fertile, moist** and **well drained**. These plants do not tolerate compacted or clay soils.

Tips

These low-growing plants make a colourful addition to the front of a border.

They are useful in a new rock garden where slower-growing alpine plants have not yet filled in.

Be careful when handling these plants; touching the leaves may cause a skin rash.

Recommended

A. arvensis (scarlet pimpernel) is a low, trailing plant that grows up to 15 cm (6") tall and spreads up to 45 cm (18"). It bears red or white flowers that close on cloudy days and at night. This species prefers cool weather and may stop flowering in summer.

A. monellii 'Skylover' (photos this page)

A. monellii (blue pimpernel) is low growing but more upright than *A. arvensis*. It grows 20–45 cm (8–18") tall, with an equal spread, and bears blue, white, pink or red flowers. This species prefers warm weather. **'Skylover'** is an upright plant from Proven Winners. It bears deep blue flowers, larger than the flowers of the species. Newly introduced **Wildcat Hybrids** are available in blue and orange. They are more compact in form and flower earlier than other hybrids.

Problems & Pests

Aphids can be a problem.

Pincushion Flower

Scabiosa

Height: 45–90 cm (18–36") **Spread:** up to 30 cm (12") **Flower colour:** purple, blue, maroon, pink, white, red; attractive foliage

PINCUSHION FLOWERS ARE LIKELY SOMETHING THAT MOST gardeners have never experienced, but they are well worth trying. The eye-catching flowers work in just about any garden design, including contemporary or cottage-style settings. If you're wondering how this unusual flower gained its infamous name, it is because the white-tipped stamens that peak out above the petals resemble tiny stick-pins. As they go to seed, these flowers transform into multicoloured orbs made up of bracts and seeds, which are perfect for everlasting floral displays. Their ever-evolving transformation is guaranteed to provide interest for at least two to three seasons, and who could possibly ask more from an annual?

Several species of annual pincushion flower, including some that are wonderfully scented, perform extremely well in northern gardens.

Planting

Seeding: Indoors in late winter; direct sow in mid-spring

Planting out: After last frost

Spacing: 30–40 cm (12–16")

Growing

Pincushion flower grows best in **full sun.** The soil should be of **average to rich fertility, alkaline, well drained** and **rich in organic matter.** Keep soil moderately moist, but do not overwater.

Tips

Pincushion flower is useful in beds, borders and mixed containers. The flowers are also popular in fresh arrangements.

The tall stems of *S. atropurpurea* may fall over as the plants mature. Insert twiggy branches, called pea sticks, into the ground around the plants when they are small to give them support as they grow.

Recommended

S. atropurpurea is an upright, branching plant growing up to 90 cm

S. stellata (above)
S. atropurpurea 'Imperial Giants' (below)

(36") tall and spreading about 30 cm (12"). Its flowers may be white, blue, purple or red. **'Imperial Giants'** bears blooms in a deep maroon colour and in shades of pink. **Olympia Hybrids** bear flowers in a wide range of colours.

S. stellata (star flower) grows 45 cm (18") tall and spreads half as much. This plant bears small, white flowers but is grown for its papery seedpods, which dry in unusual globe shapes and are useful accents in dried arrangements. Pick *S. stellata* while still slightly green to keep the dried seedpods from shattering. **'Paper Moon'** ('Drumstick') bears blue flowers that dry to a warm bronze colour.

Poppy
Papaver

Height: 30 cm–1.2 m (12"–4') **Spread:** 30 cm (12") **Flower colour:** red, pink, white, purple, yellow, orange; attractive foliage

BREATHTAKING FIELDS OF RED POPPIES AREN'T SOON FORGOTTEN and are one of the many reasons I travel to the UK each spring. Poppies are equally beautiful here at home and are regaining their former glory. Every plant experiences highs and lows in marketability, especially with the onslaught of new introductions each year. From the delicate, tissue paper-like petals that flutter in the breeze to the tough little varieties that are native to some of the coldest parts of the world, you simply can't go wrong with poppies. They have been a part of our gardening heritage for generations and will still be in our gardens long after we're gone.

Planting

Seeding: Direct sow every two weeks in spring

Spacing: 30 cm (12")

Growing

Poppies grow best in **full sun**. The soil should be **fertile** and **sandy** with **lots of organic matter** mixed in. **Good drainage** is essential.

Do not start seeds indoors because transplanting is often unsuccessful. Mix the tiny seeds with fine sand for even sowing. Do not cover, as the seeds need light for germination. Deadhead to prolong blooms.

Tips

Poppies work well in mixed borders where other plants are slow to grow.

Poppies will fill in empty spaces early in the season then die back over the summer, leaving room for other plants. They can also be used in rock gardens, and the cut flowers are popular for fresh arrangements.

P. somniferum 'Peony Flowered' (above)
P. nudicaule (below)

These fleeting beauties will not interfere with later-blooming perennials. Simply remove the spent poppies as they decline.

P. nudicaule (above)

P. somniferum cultivar (above)
P. nudicaule (below)

Be careful when weeding around faded summer plants; you may accidentally pull up late-summer poppy seedlings.

Recommended

P. nudicaule (Iceland poppy) is a short-lived perennial grown as an annual. It grows 30–45 cm (12–18") tall and 30 cm (12") wide. Red, orange, yellow, pink or white flowers appear in spring and early summer. This plant tends to self-seed, but it will gradually disappear from the garden if left to its own devices. **'Champagne Bubbles'** bears flowers in solid and bicoloured shades of red, orange and yellow.

P. rhoeas (Flanders poppy, field poppy, corn poppy) forms a basal rosette of foliage above which the flowers are borne on long stems. **'Mother of Pearl'** bears flowers in pastel pinks and purples. **Shirley Series** (Shirley poppy) has flowers in many colours. The flowers are single, semi-double or double with silky, cup-shaped petals.

P. somniferum (opium poppy) grows up to 1.2 m (4') tall. The flowers are red, pink, white or purple. This plant has a mixed reputation. Its milky sap is the source of several drugs, including codeine, morphine and opium. All parts of the plant can cause stomach upset and even coma except for the seeds, which are a popular culinary additive (poppy seeds). The seeds contain only minute amounts of the chemicals that make this plant pharmaceutically valuable. The large seed capsules are also dried and used in floral arrangements. Though propagation of the species is restricted in many countries, several attractive cultivars have been developed for ornamental use. **'Danebrog Lace'** originated in the 19th century. The single flowers have frilly, red petals with a large white patch at the base of each petal. **'Peony Flowered'** has large, frilly, double flowers in a variety of colours on plants that grow up to 90 cm (36") tall.

Problems & Pests

Poppies rarely have problems, although fungi may be troublesome if the soil is wet and poorly drained.

P. somniferum cultivar (above), *P. rhoeas* (below)

Portulaca

Portulaca

Height: 10–20 cm (4–8") **Spread:** 15–30 cm (6–12") or more
Flower colour: red, pink, yellow, white, purple, orange, peach

THERE ARE FEW OTHER ANNUALS THAT CAN TOLERATE HEAT AND dry conditions better than portulaca, especially while flowering profusely. The flowers are produced in intense, vibrant colours, and displayed on delicate petals reminiscent of brightly coloured tissue. But don't be fooled—the flowers are a sure-fire indication of this plant's tough disposition and tolerance to adverse conditions. This tolerance is partly because the leaves are succulent and store water for drier periods. Often the only thing that harms portulaca is love and the excessive watering that goes with it. Tuck this plant into the nooks and crannies along stone walls and into rock gardens, and watch it go.

With only minimal attention, portulacas will fill a sunny, exposed strip of soil next to pavement with bright colours all summer.

Planting

Seeding: Indoors in late winter

Planting out: Once soil has warmed

Spacing: 30 cm (12")

Growing

Portulaca requires **full sun**. The soil should be of **poor fertility, sandy** and **well drained**. To ensure that you will have plants where you want them, start seed indoors. If you sow directly outdoors, the tiny seeds may get washed away by rain and the plants will pop up in unexpected places. Spacing the plants close together is not a problem; in fact, the intertwining of the plants and colourful flowers creates an interesting and attractive effect.

Tips

Portulaca is the ideal plant for garden spots that just don't get enough water—under the eaves of the house or in dry, rocky, exposed areas. It is also ideal for people who like baskets hanging from the front porch but only occasionally remember to water them. As long as the location is sunny, this plant will do well with minimal care.

Recommended

P. grandiflora forms a bushy mound of succulent foliage. It bears delicate, papery, rose-like flowers profusely all summer. **'Cloudbeater'** bears large double flowers in many colours. **Duet Series** is available in two varieties; yellow on rose and red on yellow. The flowers stay open all day, even in cloudy weather. **'Sundance'** plants are low spreading with semi-double and double flowers in a wide

P. grandiflora (photos this page)

range of colours. **Sundial Series** plants have long-lasting double flowers. 'Sundial Peach' is an All-America Selections winner; it has double flowers in shades of peach. **'Yubi'** series offers a stunning array of colours in a single flower form. This award-winning series is available in white, yellow, light pink, pink, rose, red, scarlet and apricot.

Problems & Pests

If portulaca has excellent drainage and as much light as possible, it shouldn't have problems.

Salvia

Salvia

Height: 30 cm–1.2 m (1'–4') **Spread:** 20 cm–1.2 m (8"–4')
Flower colour: red, blue, purple, burgundy, pink, orange, salmon, yellow, cream, white or bicoloured; attractive foliage, apricot, salmon

THERE ARE A WIDE VARIETY OF SALVIAS ON THE MARKET. TALL salvias and small salvias, brightly coloured salvias and ones that bear flowers in muted, cool tones. They require very little attention and hold their own throughout the season. With a little deadheading, they'll produce wave after wave of flower spikes that won't fall over. The blue-flowering selections are beautiful beside ponds and water features, and cool colours bring out the best qualities of silvery leaved plants. Salvia is composed of the largest selection of blue tones on the market. This is ideal for those who have trouble growing lavender, salvia makes a reasonable substitute for gardeners who just can't live without purple-blue flower tones in the garden.

Planting

Seeding: Indoors in mid-winter; direct sow in spring

Planting out: After last frost

Spacing: 25 cm (10")

Growing

All salvias prefer **full sun** but tolerate light shade. The soil should be **moist, well drained** and of **average to rich fertility**, with **lots of organic matter**.

To keep plants producing flowers, water often and fertilize monthly. Remove spent flowers before they begin to turn brown.

Tips

Salvias look good grouped in beds, borders and containers. The flowers are long lasting and lovely in fresh arrangements.

Recommended

S. farinacea (mealy cup sage, blue sage) is a tender perennial that has bright blue flowers clustered along stems powdered with silver. The plant grows up to 60 cm (24") tall, with a spread of 30 cm (12"). The flowers are also available in white. **'Strata'** grows 35–45 cm (14–18") tall. This Fleuroselect and All-America Selections winner has a bushy, uniform and compact form, with silver flower spikes carrying small, single blue flowers. **'Victoria'** is a popular cultivar with silvery foliage and deep blue flowers that make a beautiful addition to cut-flower arrangements.

S. patens (gentian sage) bears vivid blue flowers on plants 45–60 cm

S. splendens (above), *S. farinacea* (below)

(18–24") tall. This tender perennial is grown as an annual. Being tuberous-rooted, it can be lifted and brought inside for winter in the same way that dahlias can. **'Cambridge Blue'** bears pale blue flowers.

S. splendens (salvia, scarlet sage) is an annual that grows 30–45 cm (12–18") tall and spreads up to 30 cm (12"). It is known for its spikes of bright red, tubular flowers. Recently, cultivars have become available in white, pink, purple and orange. **'Phoenix'** forms neat, compact plants with flowers in many bright and pastel shades. **'Salsa'** bears solid and bicoloured flowers in shades of red, orange, purple, burgundy, cream and pink. **Sizzler Series** plants bear flowers in burgundy, lavender, pink, plum, red, salmon, and bicoloured white and salmon. **'Vista'** is an early-flowering, compact plant with dark blue-green foliage and bright red flowers.

S. farinacea 'Victoria' (above)
S. splendens and *S. farinacea* with lobelia (below)

S. viridis (*S. horminum;* annual
clary sage) is grown for its colourful
bracts, not its flowers. It grows
45–60 cm (18–24") tall, with a
spread of 20–30 cm (8–12").
'Claryssa' grows 45 cm (18") tall
and has bracts in pink, purple, blue
or white. **'Oxford Blue'** bears purple-
blue bracts.

Problems & Pests

Seedlings are prone to damping off.
Aphids and a few fungal problems
may occur.

*The long-lasting flowers of salvias
hold up well in adverse weather.*

S. *farinacea* cultivar (above), 'Victoria' (below)

Silene
Catchfly
Silene

Height: 15–50 cm (6–20") **Spread:** 15 cm (6") **Flower colour:** pink with a white centre

SILENE IS WELL SUITED TO A WILD GARDEN OR MEADOW landscape. Once introduced, it grows vigorously and blooms prolifically until hard frost. What seed is present falls to the ground allowing for a new crop the following spring. This cycle will repeat itself for years when the seedheads are left intact. Most silene selections have single blossoms, but some produce double blooms, including *S. pendula* 'Peach Blossom' and 'Snowball'. Silene's pendent stems, clothed in colourful flowers, are showy when cascading down ugly retaining walls and rock terraces. This plant is also very pretty in a hanging basket combined with pink petunias, white bacopa or variegated ivy. The combinations are simply endless.

Planting
Seeding: Direct sow around last frost date.

Planting out: After last frost date

Spacing: 15 cm (6")

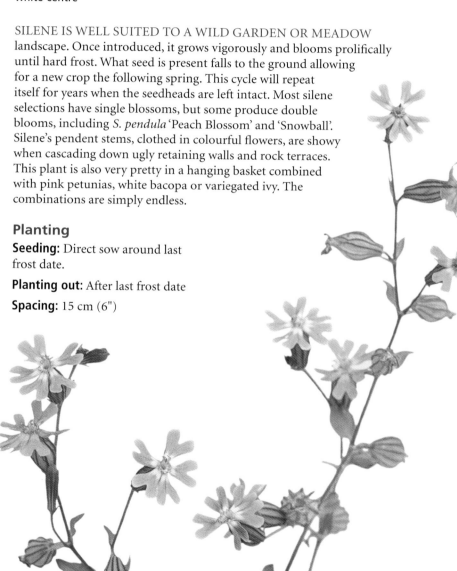

Growing

Silene grows equally well in **full sun** or **light shade**. Soil should be **fertile, moist** and **well drained**.

Tips

Silene makes a good filler plant in a shrub or mixed border. It can be included in beds, borders, planters and rock gardens. These annuals may turn up in your garden year after year, as they tend to self-seed.

Recommended

S. armeria (sweet william catchfly) forms a basal rosette of leaves from which many sticky stems emerge. It grows about 30–60 cm (12–24") tall, spreads 15–30 cm (6–12") wide and bears clusters of vivid pink flowers. **'Electra'** bears more flower clusters than the species.

S. coeli-rosa forms an upright plant with slender grey-green foliage. It grows up to 50 cm (20") tall and spreads about 15 cm (6"). Flowers are bright pink with paler, often white centres. **Angel Series** grows 15–50 cm (6–20") tall and spreads to 15 cm (6"). **'Angel Blue'** bears blue flowers. **'Angel Rose'** bears bright pink flowers.

S. pendula (nodding catchfly) is a bushy upright or spreading plant. It grows 15–30 cm (6–12") tall, with an equal spread and bears loose clusters of nodding single or double light pink flowers. **'Peach Blossom'** has double flowers that open a deep pink and gradually fade to white as they mature, with flowers in different stages of colouration showing at once. **'Snowball'** bears double white flowers.

C. pendula 'Peach Blossom' (above), *C. coeli-rosa* (below)

Problems & Pests

Aphids, snails, slugs, whitefly, rust, leaf fungus and spider mites can be a problem.

Snapdragon
Antirrhinum

Height: 15 cm–1.2 m (6"–4') **Spread:** 15–60 cm (6–24") **Flower colour:** white, cream, yellow, orange, red, maroon, pink, purple or bicoloured; attrative foliage

SNAPDRAGONS SHOULD BE A STAPLE IN EVERY PRAIRIE GARDEN. Even in hanging baskets and containers they stand up proud and carefree. Children love them because of their whimsical dragon faces. Adults love them for a variety of reasons, but mostly because they are one of the few

annuals that can go out in early spring without fear of failing after a frost. I grew one of the dwarf cultivars called 'Lampion' with great success. The flowering stems trailed over the edge of my containers and bloomed non-stop from spring to fall. Few flowers equal the beauty of snapdragons in floral arrangements, but just make sure you are not taking bees along that might be hiding inside the dragon's mouth or you're bound to be stung.

Snapdragons can handle cold weather, so they are a good choice for gardeners who can't wait until the last-frost date to plant their annuals.

Planting

Seeding: Indoors in late winter; direct sow in spring

Planting out: After last frost

Spacing: 15–45 cm (6–18")

Growing

Snapdragons prefer **full sun** but tolerate light or partial shade. The soil should be **fertile, rich in organic matter** and **well drained**. These plants prefer a neutral or alkaline soil and will not perform as well in acidic soil. Do not cover seeds when sowing because they require light for germination.

A. *majus* cultivars (photos this page)

To encourage bushy growth, pinch the tips of the young plants. Cut off the flower spikes as they fade to promote further blooming and to prevent the plant from dying back before the end of the season.

Tips

The height of the variety dictates the best place for it in a border—the shortest varieties work well near the front, and the tallest look good in the centre or at the back. The dwarf and medium-height varieties can also be used in planters, and there is even a trailing variety that does well in hanging baskets.

Snapdragons are perennials grown as annuals. They tolerate cold nights well into fall and may survive a mild winter. Self-sown seedlings may sprout the following spring if plants are left in place over winter, but because most snapdragons are hybrids, the seedlings will not come true to type.

A. majus hybrids (photos this page)

Recommended

There are many cultivars of **A. majus** available. Snapdragons are grouped into three size categories: dwarf, medium and giant.

Dwarf varieties grow up to 30 cm (12") tall. **'Floral Showers'** is a true dwarf, growing 15–20 cm (6–8") tall. This plant bears flowers in a wide range of solid colours and bicolours. **'Lampion'** is a new and interesting cultivar, usually grouped with the semi-dwarfs. It has a trailing habit and cascades up to 90 cm (36"), making it a great plant for hanging baskets. **'Princess'** bears white-and-purple bicoloured flowers. This plant produces many shoots from the base and therefore many flower spikes.

Medium snapdragons grow 30–60 cm (12–24") tall. **'Black Prince'** bears striking, dark purple-red flowers set against bronze green foliage. **'Jamaican Mist'** grows 45 cm (18") tall and produces trumpet-like flowers in pastel pink, yellow, apricot, rose and peach. **Sonnet Series** contains plants that grow to 90 cm (36") tall and are just as attractive as cut flowers as they are in the garden.

Giant or **tall cultivars** can grow 90 cm–1.2 m (3–4') tall. **'Madame Butterfly'** has double flowers in a wide range of colours. The flowers of this cultivar are open-faced with a ruffled edge and they don't 'snap' because the hinged, mouth-like structure has been lost with the addition of the extra petals. **Rocket Series** plants produce long spikes of brightly coloured flowers. The flowers come in many shades and have good heat tolerance.

Problems & Pests

Snapdragons can suffer from several fungal problems, including powdery mildew, fungal leaf spot, root rot, wilt and downy mildew. Snapdragon rust is the worst. To prevent rust, avoid wetting the foliage when watering, choose rust-resistant varieties and plant snapdragons in different parts of the garden each year. Aphids may also be troublesome.

Snapdragons are extremely sensitive to gravity, a phenomenon known as geotropism. When they are held in a horizontal position, they quickly turn upward.

A. majus hybrids (photos this page)

Statice

Limonium

Height: 30–60 cm (12–24") **Spread:** 15–30 cm (6–12") **Flower colour:** blue, purple, pink, white, yellow, red, orange, apricot, salmon

FLORAL DESIGNERS AND CRAFTERS HAVE BEEN THE BIGGEST supporters of this flowering annual. Both fresh and dried, it adds a strong visual effect to arrangements and crafts. The flower colour stays true before and after drying. Another great thing about statice is that it doesn't need to be centre stage in your mixed beds and borders. In fact it is quite happy off to the side in poorer soils. This plant is also known to thrive in excessive heat. Statice can be planted along with other everlasting annuals, including strawflower and pincushion flower. This combination will add wonderful colour in areas where you just weren't able to get the soil amended that year, or where you don't ever plan to.

Statice can make an appealing temporary hedge in dry areas of the garden where colour is often lacking.

Planting

Seeding: Indoors in mid-winter; direct sow in spring

Planting out: After last frost

Spacing: 15–30 cm (6–12")

Growing

Statice prefers **full sun**. The soil should be of **poor** or **average fertility, light, sandy** and **well drained**. This plant doesn't like having its roots disturbed, so if starting it indoors, use peat pots. Germination takes 14–21 days.

Tips

Statice makes an interesting addition to any sunny border, particularly in informal gardens. It is a perennial grown as an annual.

The basal leaves of statice form a rosette, and the flower stalks are sent up from the middle of the plant. Space the plants quite closely together to make up for this lack of width.

Cut statice for drying late in summer, before the white centre has come out on the bloom. Stand the stalks in a vase with about 2.5 cm (1") of water and they will dry quite nicely on their own as the water is used up. If it is more convenient to keep them out of the way, you can hang them upside down in a cool, dry place.

Recommended

L. sinuatum forms a basal rosette of hairy leaves. Ridged stems bear clusters of small, papery flowers in blue, purple, pink or white. **'Fortress'** has strongly branching plants and flowers

L. sinuatum cultivar

in several bright and pastel shades. The plants grow up to 60 cm (24") tall. **'Petite Bouquet'** series has compact plants, 30 cm (12") tall, with flowers in blue, purple, pink, white and yellow. **'Sunset'** grows 60 cm (24") tall and bears flowers in warm red, orange, peach, yellow, apricot and salmon shades.

Problems & Pests

Most problems can be avoided by providing a well-drained site and ensuring that there is good air circulation around the plants.

Stock

Matthiola

Height: 20–90 cm (8–36") **Spread:** 30 cm (12") **Flower colour:** pink, purple, red, rose, yellow, white

STOCKS ARE NOTED FOR THEIR FRAGRANCE AND VALUE AS A CUT flower. This old-fashioned flowering annual is native to the Mediterranean, but it has been used in traditional English cottage-style gardens for many years. The highly fragrant flowers are borne on thick stems that heartily support the 2.5 cm (1") wide or larger, double or single flowers. Stock is popular with the floral industry because of its brilliantly coloured, densely clustered flowerheads as well as its scent. In fact, certain species are grown specifically for this purpose. The flowers hold onto their colour and fragrance in the vase and on the plant for lengthy periods. It's easy to bring the outdoors inside with stocks.

When cutting stock flowers for arrangements, cut and then crush the ends of the woody stems so they will draw water more easily.

Planting

Seeding: Indoors in mid-winter; direct sow around last-frost date. Do not cover seeds because they require light to germinate.

Planting out: After last frost

Spacing: 30 cm (12")

Growing

Stocks prefer **full sun** but tolerate partial shade. The soil should be of **average fertility** with **lots of organic matter** worked in. It should also be **moist** but **well drained**. Taller plants may need to be staked.

Shelter from the hot afternoon sun helps keep these plants looking good and blooming well.

A second sowing in mid-summer may result in fall blooms when the weather cools.

Tips

Stocks can be used in mixed beds or in mass plantings.

Night-scented stock should be planted where its wonderful scent can be enjoyed in the evening—near open windows, beside patios or along pathways. It is best to place night-scented stock with other plants because it tends to look wilted and bedraggled during the day but revives impressively at night.

Recommended

M. incana (stock) has many cultivar groups. Its colours range from pink and purple to red, rose or white. The height can be 20–90 cm (8–36"), depending on the cultivar. The compact plants in **Cinderella Series** grow about 25 cm (10") tall and

M. incana (photos this page)

have fragrant, colourful flowers. The plants in **Excelsior Mammoth Column Series** grow about 90 cm (36") tall and 30 cm (12") wide. The flower spikes are up to 30 cm (12") long and bear double flowers of red, pink, light purple, pale yellow or white.

M. longipetala subsp. *bicornis* (night-scented stock, evening-scented stock) has pink or purple flowers that fill the evening air with their scent. The plants grow 30–45 cm (12–18") tall. **'Starlight Scentsation'** bears flowers in a wide range of colours.

Problems & Pests

Root rot or other fungal problems may occur. Slugs may be attracted to young foliage.

Strawflower

Everlasting

Bracteantha (Xerochrysum, Helichrysum)

Height: 30 cm–1.5 m (1–5') **Spread:** 30–60 cm (12–24")
Flower colour: yellow, red, bronze, orange, pink, white, purple

STRAWFLOWER IS ONE OF THE MOST POPULAR EVERLASTING annuals available. Similar to statice, strawflower can tolerate the driest of conditions in the brightest location in nutrient poor soils. Its flowers compliment the flowers of other everlastings, even those with cooler-coloured blooms. The flowers also dry wonderfully, holding onto their vibrant colour and form for years, hence the term everlasting. To ensure their longevity, it's important to cut the stems just as the buds are beginning to open. Remove any leaves, then hang the stems upside down in a dry location with great air circulation and no direct sunlight. In a few weeks the flowers will be ready for use.

Planting

Seeding: Indoors in early spring; direct sow after last frost. Do not cover seeds because they require light to germinate.

Planting out: After last frost

Spacing: 25–45 cm (10–18")

Growing

Strawflower prefers locations that receive **full sun**. The soil should be of **poor to average fertility, neutral to alkaline, sandy, moist** and **well drained**.

Strawflower is drought tolerant. Overwatering causes the leaves to turn yellow and encourages disease. Overly fertile soil will cause the plants to grow too tall and flop over.

Tips

Include strawflower in mixed beds, borders and containers. The lowest growing varieties make useful edging plants. Taller varieties may require staking.

Strawflower is most often used for fresh or dried flower arrangements.

Recommended

Bracteantha bracteata (*Helichrysum bracteatum*) is a tall, upright plant with grey-green foliage and brightly coloured, papery flowers. The species can grow up to 1.5 m (5') tall, but the cultivars are generally a bit more compact. **Bright Bikini Series** has compact plants that grow to about 30 cm (12") tall and bear large, colourful flowers. **'Golden Beauty'** is a Proven Winners selection. It bears bright yellow flowers and is useful in containers, hanging baskets and window boxes. **Pastel Mixed**

B. bracteata cultivar (photos this page)

has smaller flowers in soft tones that blend well with other colours. The SUNDAZE **Series** of strawflowers is the most compact to date. 'SUNDAZE BRONZE' has yellow, semi-double flowers with rusty tips and 'SUNDAZE GOLDEN BEAUTY' has mustard yellow flowers with tight centres.

Problems & Pests

Strawflower is susceptible to downy mildew.

Sunflower

Helianthus

Height: dwarf varieties 60–90 cm (24–36"); giants up to 4.5 m (15')
Spread: 30–60 cm (12–24") **Flower colour:** most commonly yellow but
also orange, red, brown, cream or bicoloured; typically with brown, purple
or rusty red centres

SUNFLOWERS ARE PROBABLY ONE OF THE MOST ENDEARING
plants to children, especially when cultivars are developed with names like
'Teddy Bear,' 'Big Smile' and 'Vanilla Ice.' There are so many sunflowers to
choose from it can be almost overwhelming. Breeders have come a long way
since the first selections that needed a ladder for harvest. Now we can choose
which fiery colour and size we prefer. *H. annuus* is grown as a crop for its
seeds, which are used for roasting, snacking, baking or for producing oil or
flour. Whether they've been planted for decorative or edible purposes, sunflowers are simply a joy to have in a prairie garden.

*Leave the plants in
the garden over the
winter for a
natural bird feeder.*

Planting

Seeding: Indoors in late winter; direct sow in spring

Planting out: After last frost

Spacing: 30–60 cm (12–24")

Growing

Sunflower grows best in **full sun**. The soil should be of **average fertility, humus rich, moist** and **well drained**.

The annual sunflower is an excellent plant for children to grow. The seeds are big and easy to handle, and they germinate quickly. The plants grow continually upwards, and their progress can be measured until the flower finally appears on top of the tall plant. If planted along the wall of a two-storey house, beneath an upstairs window, the progress can be observed from above as well as below, and the flowers will be easier to see.

H. annuus cultivar (above)
H. annuus 'Teddy Bear' (below)

Tips

The lower-growing varieties can be used in beds and borders. The tall varieties are effective at the backs of borders and make good screens and temporary hedges. The tallest varieties may need staking.

Birds will flock to the ripening seed-heads of your sunflowers, quickly

plucking out the tightly packed seeds. If you plan to keep the seeds to eat, you may need to place a mesh net, the sort used to keep birds out of cherry trees, around the flower-heads until the seeds ripen. The net can be a bit of a nuisance and isn't very attractive; most gardeners leave the flowers to the birds and buy seeds for eating.

Recommended

H. annuus (common sunflower) is considered weedy, but the development of many new cultivars has revived the use of this plant. **'Evening Sun'** produces flowers in shades of red and brown and grows 1.8–2 m (6–7') tall. **'Music Box'** is a branching plant that grows about 75 cm (30") tall and has flowers in all colours, including some bicolours. **'Prado Red'** bears deep

H. annuus cultivars (photos this page)

mahogany flowers and grows up to 1.5 m (5'). **'Russian Giant'** grows up to 3 m (10') tall and bears yellow flowers and large seeds. **'Teddy Bear'** has fuzzy-looking double flowers on compact plants 60–90 cm (24–36") tall. **'Valentine'** bears creamy yellow flowers and grows up to 1.5 m (5'). **'Velvet Queen'** is a branching cultivar that bears many crimson red flowers.

Problems & Pests

Powdery mildew may affect these plants.

Plant a row of sunflowers at the back of the vegetable garden or use one of the lower growing varieties against a split-rail fence.

H. annuus cultivars (photos this page)

Swan River Daisy

Brachyscome (Brachycome)

Height: 20–45 cm (8–18") **Spread:** equal to or slightly greater than height
Flower colour: blue, pink, white, purple; usually with yellow centres; attractive foliage

PETITE, BRIGHTLY COLOURED, PURPLE, DAISY-LIKE FLOWERS WITH bright yellow centres cover the ferny foliage of this plant in early summer. Gardeners are probably most familiar with Swan River daisies in hanging baskets and mixed containers where the mounds of flowers spill over the edges. This bushy, filler plant is also perfect for rockeries where drainage is optimal, and it is tough enough to take windy locations without fading or burning. Along with portulaca, sedum and creeping phlox, Swan River daisy can be tucked into crevices in stone or brick walls, or between stones in walkways. The foliage is soft to the touch and appears delicate and feathery, even though it is actually really tough.

The flowers are fragrant and long lasting when cut for arrangements.

Planting

Seeding: Indoors in late winter; direct sow in mid-spring

Planting out: Early spring

Spacing: 30 cm (12")

Growing

Swan River daisy prefers **full sun** but benefits from **light shade in the afternoon**. The soil should be **fertile** and **well drained**. The soil should never be waterlogged, but if mature plants dry out, they will decline rapidly.

Plant out early because cool spring weather encourages compact, sturdy growth. This plant is frost tolerant and tends to die back when the summer gets too hot.

Cut it back if it begins to fade, and don't plant it in hot areas of the garden.

Tips

Use this versatile plant for edging beds and in rock gardens, mixed containers and hanging baskets.

Combine Swan River daisy with plants that mature later in the season. As it fades in July, its companions will be filling in and beginning to flower.

Recommended

B. **hybrids** are all heat-tolerant selections. **'Blue Zephyr,'** an award-winning hybrid, produces bluish purple flowers with bright yellow centres. **'Compact Pink'** grows 22–30 cm (9–12") tall with dense, lacy foliage and light pink flowers. **'Hot Candy'** grows 15–25 cm (6–10") tall and has larger leaves than other Swan River daisies. The flowers are

B. iberidifolia (photos this page)

bright pink. **'New Amethyst'** has deep, dark purple petals, surrounding yellow centres. **'Toucan Tango'** grows 15–30 cm (6–12") tall, with an equal spread. Bright lavender to violet blue flowers bloom from late spring to fall.

B. iberidifolia forms a bushy, spreading mound of feathery foliage. Blue-purple or pink-purple flowers are borne all summer. **'Bravo'** bears white, blue, purple or pink flowers profusely in a cool but bright spot. **Splendor Series** has dark-centred flowers in pink, purple or white.

Problems & Pests

Aphids, slugs and snails cause occasional trouble for this plant.

Sweet Alyssum
Lobularia

Height: 7.5–30 cm (3–12") **Spread:** 15–60 cm (6–24") **Flower colour:** pink, purple, yellow, salmon, white, bicoloured

YOU CAN OFTEN DETECT SWEET ALYSSUM'S SCENT BEFORE YOU even see the plant. The delightful honey-scented flowers totally obscure the leaves almost all summer long. It may need a quick shear by August to reveal a new flush of growth and a sheet of colourful, scented flowers as tiny as pinheads. Sweet alyssum looks great when planted en masse or in large groups or rows along sidewalks, mixed borders, pathways and driveways. It looks beautiful snuggled up in hanging baskets or containers where you can smell it as you water. Heliotrope is only one of many fine plant companions.

Alyssum, *the original genus name for this annual, comes from Greek and means "not madness," referring to the belief that the plant could cure rabies.*

L. maritima cultivar

Planting

Seeding: Indoors in late winter; direct sow in spring

Planting out: Once soil has warmed

Spacing: 20–30 cm (8–12")

Growing

Sweet alyssum prefers **full sun** but tolerates light shade. **Well-drained** soil with **average fertility** is preferred, but poor soil is tolerated. This plant dislikes having its roots disturbed, so if starting it indoors, use peat pots or pellets. Trim sweet alyssum back occasionally over the summer to keep it flowering and looking good.

Leave sweet alyssum plants out all winter. In spring, remove the previous year's growth to expose self-sowed seedlings below.

Tips

Sweet alyssum will creep around rock gardens, on rock walls and along the edges of beds. It is an excellent choice for seeding into cracks and crevices of walkway and patio stones, and once established it readily re-seeds. It is also good for filling in spaces between taller plants in borders and mixed containers.

Recommended

L. maritima forms a low, spreading mound of foliage. The entire plant appears to be covered in tiny blossoms when it is in full flower. '**Pastel Carpet**' bears flowers in rose, white, violet and mauve. '**Snow Crystal**' bears large, bright white flowers profusely all summer. **Wonderland Series** offers a mix of all colours on compact plants.

Problems & Pests

Alyssum rarely has problems but is sometimes afflicted with downy mildew.

Sweet Pea

Lathyrus

Height: 30 cm–1.8 m (1–6') **Spread:** 15–30 cm (6–12") **Flower colour:** pink, red, purple, blue, salmon, pale yellow, peach, white or bicoloured

ONE OF THE MANY REASONS WE CAN GROW SWEET PEAS ON THE prairies is because of our cool nights. They're relatively easy to grow but the following methods will ensure their success. Treat the seed with pea inoculant before sowing to be sure the plant will form root nodules enabling it to fix nitrogen from the air to the soil. You should not plant peas where they grew last year, but, if you grew peas successfully in the spot two or more years back, the soil should already contain the bacteria, so inoculation is unnecessary. If they're grown in the same location for years, the soil may become depleted and the plants will become stunted, thin and will bloom less.

Sweet peas are attractive and long lasting as cut flowers. The more sweet pea flowers you cut, the more the plant will bloom.

Planting

Seeding: Direct sow in early spring

Spacing: 15–30 cm (6–12")

Growing

Sweet pea prefers **full sun** but tolerates light shade. The soil should be **fertile, high in organic matter, moist** and **well drained**. Fertilize very lightly with a low-nitrogen fertilizer during the flowering season. Adding compost or well-rotted manure annually is also beneficial. This plant will tolerate light frost. Deadhead all spent blooms.

Soak seeds in water for 24 hours or nick them with a nail file before planting them. Planting a second crop of sweet pea about a month after the first one will ensure a longer blooming period.

Tips

Sweet pea will grow up poles, trellises and fences or over rocks. The low-growing varieties form low, shrubby mounds.

To help prevent disease from afflicting your sweet pea plants, avoid planting in the same location two years in a row.

It's helpful to pinch the plants back when they reach a 10 cm (4") height to encourage strong side branching and pinch off blooms once they're finished to encourage more flowers.

Recommended

Many cultivars of **L. odoratus** are available. **Bijou Series** is a popular heat-resistant variety that grows 45 cm (18") tall, with an equal spread. It needs no support to grow. **'Blue Ripple'** is a newly developed

L. odoratus cultivars

tall climber. The colour combination is totally unique, displaying creamy white flowers with blue, rippled edges. **Bouquet Mix** is a tall, climbing variety that comes in a wide array of colours and is frequently used for cut flowers. Unlike the better-known climbing type, **'Cupid'** forms a compact mound 15 cm (6") tall by 45 cm (18"). The plants bear pale pink flowers with crisp white edges. **'Sugar 'n' Spice'** was developed for its bushy trailing habit, which is ideally suited to hanging baskets. This cultivar is best suited to containers. **Supersnoop Series** is a sturdy bush type that needs no support. The flowers are fragrant. Pinch the tips of its long stems to encourage low growth.

Problems & Pests

Slugs and snails may eat the foliage of young plants. Root rot, mildew, rust and leaf spot may also afflict sweet pea occasionally.

Sweet Potato Vine

Ipomoea

Height: 60 cm–1.5 m (2–5') **Spread:** about 30 cm–1.2 m (1–4') but variable **Flower colour:** white, blue, pink, red, yellow, orange, purple, sometimes bicoloured; grown for foliage

AN ORNAMENTAL RELATIVE TO THE POTATO, SWEET POTATO VINE is grown strictly for its colourful, dense foliage. The distinctive maple leaf shape of the cultivar *I.* 'Blackie' is what drew the garden industry in, and from there the market opened up to what we have today. Cultivars are now available in deep, dark purples to yellows and chartreuse, and there are even brightly coloured variegated white, pink and green selections. Proven Winners has led the race to introduce new colourful cultivars; watch for 'Spilt Milk' and the Sweet Caroline series. Sweet potato vine creates a wonderful effect in containers and hanging baskets, spilling over the edges with great abandon. The colours play perfectly off one another and other contrasting plants, including blood grasses, amaranth, coleus and others.

Planting

Seeding: Indoors in early spring; direct sow after last frost

Planting out: Late spring

Spacing: 30–45 cm (12–18")

Growing

Sweet potato vine prefers to grow in **full sun**. Any soil will do, but a **light, well-drained** mix of **poor to average fertility** is preferred.

Tips

Sweet potato vine is the perfect specimen for containers, where it can show off its best attribute: colourful, dense, trailing stems. The dark-coloured cultivars complement vividly coloured plants, such as coleus, variegated geraniums, petunias and verbena. Conversely, the cultivar with chartreuse foliage is stunning when grown with dark, contrasting flower and foliage colours.

Recommended

I. batatas (sweet potato vine) is a twining climber that is grown for its attractive foliage rather than its flowers. Often used in planters and

I. batatas 'Tricolor' (above)
I. batatas 'Margarita' (below)

hanging baskets, it can be grown by itself or mixed with other plants. **'Black Heart'** has heart shaped, dark purple leaves. **'Blackie'** vigorously produces dark purple (almost black), deeply lobed leaves. **'Bronze'** produces deeply lobed bronze foliage with a trailing but compact habit. **'Margarita'** has yellow-green foliage on fairly compact plants. This cascading plant can also be trained to grow up a trellis. **'Tricolor'** has green, white and pink variegated foliage.

Problems & Pests

Sweet potato vine is susceptible to several fungal problems, but they occur only rarely.

Toadflax

Linaria

Height: 22.5–60 cm (9–24") **Spread:** 15 cm (6") **Flower colour:** white, pink, violet-purple, lavender-purple, rose-pink, salmon-pink, orange, yellow, deep red

THE FLOWERS OF TOADFLAX ARE VERY SIMILAR TO SNAPDRAGONS and the colours are just as bright and cheerful. Toadflax is not a new annual to the market, having been around since 1872, but is highly underused in our gardens. This often happens when there is an onslaught of new plants each year, but some of the oldies are goodies for a reason. Toadflax is quite fond of our soils, both clay and sandy based, and it responds well to long, bright summer days. It is a great substitute for other annuals with tall flowering spikes, such as snapdragons and salvia. So if you're looking for something that you've never grown before, give toadflax a try. You won't be disappointed.

Planting

Seeding: Sow seeds in the garden in early spring

Planting out: Spring or fall

Spacing: 10–15 cm (4–6")

Growing

Toadflax prefers to grow in **full sun**. Soil should be **sandy, low to moderately fertile** and **well drained**.

Tips

These wispy plants are most effective when planted en masse. They are good in the rock garden as well as in an annual or mixed border.

You may wish to remove the flower spikes as they fade. These plants self-seed very easily and you may find them growing a bit too high if you don't do something to prevent it.

Recommended

L. maroccana is an erect, sticky plant growing 22.5–45 cm (9–18") tall and 15 cm (6") wide. The two-lipped flowers bloom in summer and are violet-purple or occasionally pink or white, with the lower lip marked with orange to yellow. **'Fairy Bouquet'** produces abundant blooms in yellow, rose-pink, salmon-pink, orange, deep red, lavender-purple and white on 22.5 cm (9") tall plants. **'Fantasy Mix'** grows 15–30 cm (6–12") tall and comes in a wide range of colours and bicolours including lavender, pink, rose, yellow and white. **'Northern Lights'** grows to 60 cm (24") tall. It flowers in the same

L. maroccana

colours as 'Fairy Bouquet' and blooms for a longer period.

Problems & Pests

Occasional problems with aphids, flea beetles, downy mildew, white smut and anthracnose are possible.

The species name, maroccana, *denotes the plant's origin in Morocco.*

Verbena
Garden Verbena
Verbena

Height: 20 cm–1.5 m (8"–5') **Spread:** 25–90 cm (10–36")
Flower colour: red, pink, purple, blue, yellow, scarlet, salmon, magenta,
silver, peach, white; usually with white centres; attractive foliage

VERBENA ADDS TEXTURE AND COLOUR TO BASKETS AND CONTAINERS,
bearing clusters of flowers with coarse, bright foliage that dances above the
container's edge. Butterflies find verbena irresistible when hunting for nectar. Breeders have been busily creating new and improved selections with
even brighter colours and mildew-resistant foliage. Dwarf varieties are also
now available for uses other than in containers.
These varieties are perfectly suited to rockeries and mixed beds, where they will grow
without trailing throughout and taking
over. All in all, there's a verbena for
every garden setting and almost
every purpose. You will quickly
become a verbena convert once
you begin working with this plant.

*The Romans believed verbena
could rekindle the flames of dying
love. They named it* Herba
Veneris, *"plant of Venus."*

Planting

Seeding: Indoors in mid-winter

Planting out: After last frost

Spacing: 25–45 cm (10–18")

Growing

Verbenas grow best in **full sun**. The soil should be **fertile** and **very well drained**. Pinch back young plants for bushy growth.

Chill seeds one week before sowing. Moisten the soil before sowing seeds. Do not cover the seeds with soil. Place the entire seed tray or pot in darkness, and water only if the soil becomes very dry. Once the seeds germinate, move them into the light.

Tips

Use verbenas on rock walls and in beds, borders, rock gardens, containers, hanging baskets and window boxes. They make good

V. x hybrida Tapien Series (above)
V. x hybrida (below)

substitutes for ivy-leaved geranium where the sun is hot and where a roof overhang keeps the mildew-prone verbenas dry.

Recommended

V. bonariensis forms a low clump of foliage from which tall, stiff, flower-bearing stems emerge. The small purple flowers are held in clusters.

V. bonariensis (photos this page)

This plant grows up to 1.5 m (5') tall but spreads only 45–60 cm (18–24"). This species may survive a mild winter, and it will self-seed. Butterflies love this plant.

V. x *hybrida* is a bushy plant that may be upright or spreading. It bears clusters of small flowers in shades of white, purple, blue, pink, red or yellow. **Aztec Series** from Simply Beautiful grows 40–45 cm (16–18") tall and 25–30 cm (10–12") wide and flowers in an impressive array of purples, pinks, reds and white. **'Imagination'** (*V. x speciosa* 'Imagination') is a spreading plant that grows 30–45 cm (12–18") tall and 60–90 cm (24–36") wide. This All-America Selections winner produces clusters of intense violet-blue flowers. **'Peaches and Cream'** is a spreading plant with flowers that open to a soft peach colour and fade to white. **Romance Series** has red, pink, purple or white flowers, with white eyes. The plants grow 20–25 cm (8–10") tall. **'Showtime'** bears brightly coloured flowers on compact plants that grow to 25 cm (10") tall and spread 45 cm (18"). **Tapien Series** from Proven Winners grows 10–15 cm (4–6") tall and 25–45 cm (10–18") wide. These low-growing, well-branched plants flower in white and shades of pink and purple. **Temari Series** is mildew resistant and heat tolerant with vigorous, spreading growth. Flowers come in a range of colours on plants 20–35 cm (8–14") tall.

V. *pendula* Superbena Series are vigorous plants with an upright to trailing habit. This series from Proven Winners grows 15–30 cm

(6–12") tall and 25–35 cm (10–14") wide, boasting large flowers and excellent mildew resistance. The flowers bloom in intense shades of red, pink and purple.

Problems & Pests

Aphids, whiteflies, slugs and snails may be troublesome. Avoid fungal problems by making sure there is good air circulation around verbena plants.

The Verbena *genus consists of about 200 hardy and tender perennials, some of which are semi-evergreen. They are natives of North and South America.*

V. bonariensis (photos this page)

Vinca
Myrtle, Periwinkle
Vinca

Height: 10–20 cm (4–8") **Spread:** indefinite **Flower colour:** blue, purple, white; attractive foliage

THIS DROUGHT-TOLERANT GROUP OF PLANTS IS A GREAT CHOICE for containers because the soil in pots often dries out so quickly. Aside from their tolerance of neglect, vincas are one of the quintessential trailing annuals, along with ivy, bacopa and Swan River daisy. Mix vinca with geraniums, marigolds, petunias and salvia. They are also commonly used in hanging baskets. *V. minor* is hardy to zone 4 and may be transplanted into the ground where a groundcover is necessary, but make sure that this area is sheltered so the plant will successfully overwinter. An insulative mulch is often beneficial. Most other species and cultivars are not winter hardy, so enjoy what they have to offer throughout the warm days of summer.

The glossy green foliage of vinca remains attractive and cooling in the heat of summer, long after the early flush of flowers has finished.

Planting

Seeding: Not recommended

Planting out: Spring or fall

Spacing: 60–90 cm (24–36")

Growing

Grow vinca in **partial to full shade**. It will grow in any type of soil as long as it is not too dry. The plants turn yellow if the soil is too dry or the sun is too hot. Divide vinca in early spring or mid- to late fall, whenever it becomes overgrown.

After planting, mulch the soil surface with shredded leaves and compost to prevent weeds from sprouting among the groundcover. The mulch will also help keep the soil moist to hasten vinca's establishment and to encourage it to fill in quickly.

Tips

Vinca is a useful and attractive groundcover in a shrub border, under trees or on a shady bank, and it prevents soil erosion. Vinca is shallow-rooted and able to outcompete weeds, but it won't interfere with deeper-rooted shrubs.

If vinca begins to outgrow its space, shear it back hard in early spring. If the sheared-off ends have rooted along the stems, these cuttings may be potted and given away as gifts or may be introduced to new areas of the garden.

Recommended

V. major (blue buttons, greater periwinkle) is a trailing vine with arching shoots and dark green leaves. Bluish purple flowers are produced in mid-summer. The trailing stems

V. minor

can grow 45–60 cm (18–24") long. **'Variegata'** ('Elegantissima,' Vinca Vine) is more often available than the species and produces creamy white and green variegated foliage and violet flowers.

V. minor (creeping myrtle, lesser periwinkle) forms a low, loose mat of trailing stems. Purple or blue flowers are borne in a flush in spring and then sporadically all summer and into fall. **'Alba'** bears white flowers. **'Atropurpurea'** bears reddish purple flowers. **'Blue and Gold'** has vibrant bluish purple flowers and medium green leaves with wide edges of bright golden yellow. **'Bowles'** bears large purple-blue flowers. **'Illumination'** produces yellow and green variegated foliage. **'Ralph Shugert'** has dark, glossy, silver-edged leaves and bears purple-blue flowers that are larger than those of the species.

Wishbone Flower
Blue Wings
Torenia

Height: 15–30 cm (6–12") **Spread:** 15–30 cm (6–12") **Flower colour:** purple, pink, blue, burgundy, white; often bicoloured with a yellow spot on the lower petal

ONE OF THE FEW ANNUAL BEDDING PLANTS THAT CAN TOLERATE both sun and shade is wishbone flower. It grows into a tight, compact mat of foliage covered in colourful flowers, offering a little whimsy to the garden. There was little happening in the world of the wishbone flower for many years, but that has all changed. The Catalina and Summer Wave series have raised the bar with richly coloured, solid, bicoloured or tricoloured flowers. Often the bicoloured flowers have a touch of bright yellow at the base of the throat, like a beacon to all bees and pollinating insects. All it takes is an example of wishbone flower growing in a hanging basket by itself, resembling a green and blue, purple or pink orb, and you'll be hooked for good.

Planting

Seeding: Indoors in late winter

Planting out: After last frost

Spacing: About 20 cm (8")

Growing

Wishbone flower prefers **light shade** but tolerates partial and full shade. The soil should be **fertile, light, humus rich** and **moist**. This plant requires regular watering.

Don't cover seeds when planting; they require light to germinate.

T. fournieri (photos this page)

Tips

Wishbone flower can be massed in a shaded bed or border, used as an edging plant or added to mixed containers and hanging baskets. It makes a nice change in shade gardens if you are tired of using impatiens. Try wishbone flower near a water feature, where the soil may remain moist for extended periods.

Recommended

T. fournieri is a bushy, rounded to upright plant. It grows up to 30 cm (12") tall, with an equal or lesser spread. Its purple flowers have yellow throats. **Catalina Hybrids** are a new, more compact group that are available in blue, pink and purple. The flowers display yellow throats in bicoloured blooms. **Clown Series** features compact plants that grow 15–20 cm (6–8") tall. The flowers may be purple, blue, pink or white. **Duchess Series** has compact plants, up to 15 cm (6") tall, and bears larger flowers in a range of colours. Another new series on the market are the **Summer Wave Hybrids**. **'Summer Wave Amethyst Improved'**

has deeper, richer, purple-burgundy hued flowers, while **'Summer Wave Blue'** produces blue flowers with a violet tint. **'Summer Wave Large Violet'** bears larger, deep violet flowers and firmer, larger, and more distinctly serrated foliage.

Problems & Pests

Fungal problems can occur in overly wet soils. Moist but not soggy soils are ideal.

Zinnia

Zinnia

Height: 15–90 cm (6–36") **Spread:** 30 cm (12") **Flower colour:** red, yellow, green, purple, orange, pink, white, maroon, brown, gold

MOST GARDENERS GREW UP WITH THIS TRADITIONAL ANNUAL as children. Although zinnia flowers closely resemble other flowering annuals, like calendula or pot marigold, they also display their own unique qualities. If I was forced to find fault with this plant, it would be its tendency to fail once hot summer weather sets in. Thankfully, heat-tolerant varieties have been bred as a solution to this problem. New cultivars now enable us to appreciate the zinnia right through the growing season, without a fading bloom. Gardeners can now enjoy these flowers in all their glory, and for everything they bring to the garden.

Planting

Seeding: Indoors in late winter; direct sow after last frost

Planting out: After last frost

Spacing: 15–30 cm (6–12")

Growing

Zinnias grow best in **full sun**. The soil should be **fertile, rich in organic matter, moist** and **well drained**. When starting seeds indoors, plant them in individual peat pots to avoid disturbing the roots when transplanting.

Deadhead zinnias to keep them flowering and looking their best. To keep mildew from the leaves and botrytis blight from the flowers, plant varieties that are resistant to these problems and avoid wetting the plants when you water.

Tips

Zinnias are useful in beds, borders, containers and cutting gardens. The dwarf varieties can be used as edging plants. These plants are wonderful for fall colour. Combine the rounded zinnia flowers with the spiky blooms of sun-loving salvia, or use the taller varieties in front of sunflowers.

Recommended

Z. angustifolia (narrow-leaf zinnia) is a low, mounding plant that bears yellow and orange flowers. **'Crystal White'** bears white flowers on plants that grow 15–20 cm (6–8") tall. It makes a wonderful edger for beds and borders.

Z. elegans and its cultivars bear flowers in several forms, including single, double and cactus flowered, where the petals appear to be rolled into tubes like the spines of a cactus. **'Dreamland'** bears large double flowers up to 10 cm (4") wide on plants about 25 cm (10") tall.

Z. elegans cultivars

Thumbelina Series has small flowers in all colours on dwarf, 15 cm (6") tall, weather-resistant plants.

Z. **Profusion Series** includes fast-growing, mildew-resistant hybrids. The compact plants grow 25–45 cm (10–18") tall and bear flowers in bright cherry red, orange or white; the individual cultivars are called **'Profusion Cherry,' 'Profusion Orange'** and **'Profusion White.'**

Problems & Pests

Zinnias are prone to mildew and other fungal problems. Prevent such problems by ensuring good air circulation and drainage.

Though zinnias are quite drought tolerant, they will grow best if watered thoroughly when the soil dries out. Use a soaker hose to avoid wetting the leaves.

Quick Reference Chart

HEIGHT LEGEND: Low: < 30 cm (12")-•-Medium: 30–60 cm (12–24")-•-Tall: > 60 cm (24")

SPECIES by Common Name	White	Pink	Red	Orange	Yellow	Blue	Purple	Green	Foliage	Indoors	Direct	Low	Medium	Tall
African Daisy	•	•	•	•	•		•			•	•	•	•	
Ageratum		•				•	•			•	•	•	•	•
Amaranth			•		•			•	•	•	•			•
Angelonia	•	•				•	•						•	
Asarina	•	•	•			•	•		•	•	•		•	•
Baby's Breath	•	•					•			•	•	•	•	•
Bachelor's Buttons	•	•	•			•	•			•	•		•	
Bacopa	•	•					•					•		
Beefsteak Plant									•				•	
Bidens				•					•	•	•		•	
California Poppy		•	•	•	•				•		•	•	•	
Calla Lily	•	•	•	•	•		•		•	•	•		•	•
Candytuft	•	•	•				•			•	•	•		
Canna Lily		•	•	•	•				•	•	•			•
Cape Daisy	•	•	•	•	•				•	•	•		•	
China Aster	•	•	•	•	•	•	•			•	•	•	•	•
Cigar Flower	•	•	•				•	•		•		•	•	
Cleome	•	•					•		•	•	•		•	•
Clover	•								•			•		
Cobbitty Daisy	•	•		•	•		•		•	•	•		•	
Coleus							•		•	•	•	•	•	•
Corn Cockle	•	•					•			•	•		•	•
Cosmos	•	•	•	•	•		•		•	•	•		•	•
Cup-and-Saucer Vine	•					•	•	•	•	•				•
Cup Flower	•					•	•			•		•		
Dahlberg Daisy				•	•				•	•	•	•		
Dianthus	•	•	•				•			•	•	•		
Dwarf Morning Glory	•	•				•	•			•	•	•	•	
Fan Flower						•	•		•	•		•		
Feverfew	•	•	•		•		•		•			•	•	•

Quick Reference Chart

Hardy	Half-hardy	Tender	Sun	Part Shade	Light Shade	Shade	Moist	Well Drained	Dry	Fertile	Average	Poor	Page Number	SPECIES by Common Name
		•	•					•		•			48	African Daisy
		•	•				•	•		•			50	Ageratum
		•	•					•			•	•	54	Amaranth
		•	•				•	•		•			58	Angelonia
		•	•	•	•		•	•		•	•		60	Asarina
	•	•	•					•				•	62	Baby's Breath
•		•	•				•	•		•			64	Bachelor's Buttons
		•		•			•	•		•	•		66	Bacopa
		•	•	•			•	•					68	Beefsteak Plant
	•		•				•	•		•	•		70	Bidens
•			•					•			•	•	72	California Poppy
	•		•				•	•		•			74	Calla Lily
•			•	•				•			•	•	78	Candytuft
	•		•				•	•		•			82	Canna Lily
		•	•				•	•			•		84	Cape Daisy
		•	•	•			•	•		•			86	China Aster
		•	•	•				•		•			88	Cigar Flower
	•		•	•			•	•	•	•	•	•	92	Cleome
•			•	•			•	•					96	Clover
	•		•	•				•		•			98	Cobbitty Daisy
		•		•	•		•	•		•	•		100	Coleus
	•		•					•				•	104	Corn Cockle
		•	•					•			•	•	106	Cosmos
		•	•				•	•			•		110	Cup-and-Saucer Vine
•			•	•			•	•			•		112	Cup Flower
•			•					•			•	•	114	Dahlberg Daisy
•			•					•		•			116	Dianthus
		•	•					•			•	•	120	Dwarf Morning Glory
		•	•		•		•	•			•		122	Fan Flower
	•		•					•					124	Feverfew

Quick Reference Chart

HEIGHT LEGEND: Low: < 30 cm (12")-•-Medium: 30–60 cm (12–24")-•-Tall: > 60 cm (24")

SPECIES by Common Name	White	Pink	Red	Orange	Yellow	Blue	Purple	Green	Foliage	Indoors	Direct	Low	Medium	Tall
Flowering Flax	•	•	•			•	•				•		•	•
Flowering Maple	•	•	•	•	•					•			•	•
Forget-Me-Not	•	•				•				•	•	•		
Fountain Grass					•		•		•	•	•			•
Four-O'Clock Flower	•	•	•		•		•			•	•		•	•
Fuchsia	•	•	•	•			•					•	•	•
Gaura	•	•							•	•			•	•
Gazania	•	•	•	•	•				•	•	•	•	•	
Geranium	•	•	•	•			•		•	•		•	•	•
Globe Amaranth	•	•	•				•			•		•	•	•
Godetia	•	•	•				•				•	•	•	•
Heliotrope	•					•	•		•	•		•	•	•
Hollyhock	•	•	•		•		•		•	•				•
Hyacinth Bean	•						•		•	•	•			•
Ice Plant	•	•	•				•		•	•	•	•		
Impatiens	•	•	•	•	•		•		•	•		•	•	•
Lantana	•	•	•	•	•		•		•	•			•	
Larkspur	•	•				•	•			•	•		•	•
Lavatera	•	•	•				•		•	•	•		•	•
Licorice Plant	•				•				•				•	
Lobelia	•	•	•			•	•		•	•		•		
Lotus Vine			•	•	•				•			•		
Love-in-a-Mist	•	•				•	•		•	•	•		•	
Madagascar Periwinkle	•	•	•		•		•		•	•			•	
Maidenhair Vine									•			•		
Mexican Sunflower			•	•	•					•	•		•	•
Mignonette					•			•	•	•	•		•	
Million Bells	•	•	•	•	•	•	•		•			•		
Nemesia	•	•	•	•	•	•	•		•	•		•	•	
Nemophila	•					•	•		•		•	•		

Quick Reference Chart

Hardy	Half-hardy	Tender	Sun	Part Shade	Light Shade	Shade	Moist	Well Drained	Dry	Fertile	Average	Poor	Page Number	SPECIES by Common Name
•			•					•			•		126	Flowering Flax
		•	•				•	•		•	•		128	Flowering Maple
•					•	•	•	•		•			130	Forget-Me-Not
•			•					•			•		132	Fountain Grass
		•	•					•		•			134	Four-O'Clock Flower
		•			•	•	•	•		•			136	Fuchsia
	•		•				•	•		•			140	Gaura
		•	•					•			•	•	142	Gazania
		•	•					•		•			144	Geranium
		•	•					•			•		148	Globe Amaranth
•			•		•			•			•	•	150	Godetia
		•	•				•	•		•			152	Heliotrope
•			•					•		•	•		154	Hollyhock
	•		•				•	•		•			156	Hyacinth Bean
		•	•					•			•	•	158	Ice Plant
		•			•	•	•	•		•			160	Impatiens
	•		•				•	•		•			164	Lantana
•			•		•			•		•			166	Larkspur
•			•					•			•		168	Lavatera
	•		•					•			•	•	170	Licorice Plant
•					•	•	•	•		•			172	Lobelia
	•		•	•				•		•	•		174	Lotus Vine
•			•					•			•		176	Love-in-a-Mist
		•	•					•		•	•	•	178	Madagascar Periwinkle
•			•		•			•		•	•		180	Maidenhair Vine
		•	•					•		•	•	•	182	Mexican Sunflower
	•		•	•				•			•		184	Mignonette
	•		•				•	•		•			186	Million Bells
		•	•				•	•		•	•		188	Nemesia
•				•	•		•	•		•			190	Nemophila

Quick Reference Chart

HEIGHT LEGEND: Low: < 30 cm (12")-•-Medium: 30–60 cm (12–24")-•-Tall: > 60 cm (24")

SPECIES by Common Name	White	Pink	Red	Orange	Yellow	Blue	Purple	Green	Foliage	Indoors	Direct	Low	Medium	Tall
Ornamental Cabbage									•		•		•	
Osteospermum	•	•		•	•		•			•			•	
Oxalis	•	•			•				•	•		•		
Painted Tongue		•	•	•	•					•	•		•	
Pansy	•	•	•	•	•	•	•			•		•		
Passion Flower	•	•				•	•		•					•
Pentas	•	•	•				•		•	•			•	•
Persian Shield						•			•				•	•
Petunia	•	•	•		•	•	•			•		•	•	
Pimpernel	•	•	•			•				•		•	•	
Pincushion Flower	•	•	•			•	•		•	•	•		•	•
Poppy	•	•	•	•	•		•		•		•		•	•
Portulaca	•	•	•	•	•		•		•	•		•		
Salvia	•	•	•	•		•	•		•	•	•		•	•
Silene	•	•									•	•	•	
Snapdragon	•	•	•	•	•		•		•	•		•	•	•
Statice	•	•	•	•	•	•	•			•	•		•	
Stock	•	•	•				•			•	•	•	•	•
Strawflower	•	•	•	•	•					•	•		•	•
Sunflower			•	•	•					•	•			•
Swan River Daisy	•	•				•	•		•	•	•	•	•	
Sweet Alyssum	•	•		•	•		•			•	•	•		
Sweet Pea	•	•	•		•	•	•				•		•	•
Sweet Potato Vine							•		•	•	•	•		
Toadflax	•	•	•	•	•		•			•		•	•	
Verbena	•	•	•	•	•	•	•		•	•		•	•	•
Vinca	•	•	•				•			•			•	
Wishbone Flower	•	•	•		•	•	•			•		•		
Zinnia	•	•	•	•	•		•	•		•	•	•	•	•

Quick Reference Chart

Hardy	Half-hardy	Tender	Sun	Part Shade	Light Shade	Shade	Moist	Well Drained	Dry	Fertile	Average	Poor	Page Number	SPECIES by Common Name
•			•				•	•		•			192	Ornamental Cabbage
	•		•				•	•			•		194	Osteospermum
•	•		•	•				•		•	•		198	Oxalis
		•	•					•		•			200	Painted Tongue
•			•				•	•		•			202	Pansy
•			•	•			•	•			•		206	Passion Flower
	•		•				•	•		•			208	Pentas
		•	•	•				•		•	•		210	Persian Shield
	•		•					•		•	•		212	Petunia
		•	•				•	•		•			216	Pimpernel
	•		•					•		•	•		218	Pincushion Flower
•			•					•		•			220	Poppy
		•	•					•				•	224	Portulaca
	•		•				•	•		•	•		226	Salvia
	•		•		•		•	•		•			230	Silene
	•		•					•		•			232	Snapdragon
		•	•					•			•	•	236	Statice
•			•				•	•			•		238	Stock
	•		•				•	•			•	•	240	Strawflower
•			•				•	•			•		242	Sunflower
	•		•		•			•		•			246	Swan River Daisy
•			•					•			•		248	Sweet Alyssum
•			•				•	•		•			250	Sweet Pea
		•	•	•	•		•	•			•		252	Sweet Potato Vine
		•	•					•			•	•	254	Toadflax
•		•	•					•		•			256	Verbena
		•	•					•					260	Vinca
		•			•		•			•			262	Wishbone Flower
		•	•				•	•		•			264	Zinnia

Glossary

Acid soil: soil with a pH lower than 7.0

Alkaline soil: soil with a pH higher than 7.0

Basal leaves: leaves that form from the crown

Basal rosette: a ring or rings of leaves growing from the crown of a plant at or near ground level; flowering stems of such plants grow separately from the crown

Crown: the part of a plant where the shoots join the roots, at or just below soil level

Cultivar: a cultivated (bred) plant variety with one or more distinct differences from the parent species, e.g., in flower colour, leaf variegation or disease resistance

Damping off: fungal disease causing seedlings to rot at soil level and topple over

Deadhead: to remove spent flowers to maintain a neat appearance and encourage a longer blooming period

Direct sow: to plant seeds straight into the garden, in the location you want the plants to grow

Disbud: to remove some flower buds to improve the size or quality of the remaining ones

Dormancy: a period of plant inactivity, usually during winter or other unfavourable climatic conditions

Double flower: a flower with an unusually large number of petals, often caused by mutation of the stamens into petals

Genus: category of biological classification between the species and family levels; the first word in a scientific name indicates the genus, e.g., *Digitalis* in *Digitalis purpurea*

Hardy: capable of surviving unfavourable conditions, such as cold weather

Humus: decomposed or decomposing organic material in the soil

Hybrid: a plant resulting from natural or human-induced crossbreeding between varieties, species or genera; the hybrid expresses features of each parent plant

Invasive: able to spread aggressively from the planting site and outcompete other plants

Knot garden: a formal design, often used for herb gardens, in which low, clipped hedges are arranged in elaborate, knot-like patterns

Marginal: plants that grow in shallow water or in consistently moist soil along the edges of ponds and rivers

Neutral soil: soil with a pH of 7.0

Node: the area on a stem from which a leaf or new shoot grows

Offset: a young plantlet that naturally sprouts around the base of the parent plant in some species

pH: a measure of acidity or alkalinity (the lower the pH, the higher the acidity); the pH of soil influences availability of nutrients for plants

Rhizome: a root-like, usually swollen stem that grows horizontally underground, and from which shoots and true roots emerge

Rootball: the root mass and surrounding soil of a container-grown plant or a plant dug out of the ground

Rosette: see Basal rosette

Self-seeding: reproducing by means of seeds without human assistance, so that new plants constantly replace those that die

Semi-hardy: a plant capable of surviving the climatic conditions of a given region if protected

Semi-double flower: a flower with petals that form two or three rings

Single flower: a flower with a single ring of typically four or five petals

Species: the original plant from which a cultivar is derived; the fundamental unit of biological classification, indicated by a two-part scientific name, e.g., *Digitalis purpurea* (*purpurea* is the specific epithet)

Sport: an atypical plant or part of a plant that arises through mutation; some sports are horticulturally desirable and propagated as new cultivars

Subshrub: a perennial plant that is somewhat shrubby, with a woody basal stem; its upper parts are herbaceous and die back each year

Subspecies (subsp.): a naturally occurring, regional form of a species, often isolated from other subspecies but still potentially interfertile with them

Taproot: a root system consisting of one main vertical root with smaller roots branching from it

Tender: incapable of surviving the climatic conditions of a given region; requiring protection from frost or cold

True: describes the passing of desirable characteristics from the parent plant to seed-grown offspring; also called breeding true to type

Tuber: a swollen part of a rhizome or root, containing food stores for the plant

Variegation: describes foliage that has more than one colour, often patched or striped or bearing differently coloured leaf margins

Variety (var.): a naturally occurring variant of a species; below the level of subspecies in biological classification; also applied to forms produced in cultivation, which are properly called cultivars

Feverfew

Sunflower

Index

Boldface type indicates main plant entries.